Entrepreneurial Min Mastering the Mental Game of Business Success

Michael Allen
First Edition | 2025

Dedicated to every scrappy underdog with something to prove.

Entrepreneurial Mindset:
Mastering the Mental Game of Business Success

For permission requests, contact the publisher at:

Michael@epr-sc.com

This book is a work of nonfiction. All stories and experiences are true to the best of the author's knowledge. Some names and identifying details may have been changed to protect privacy.

Author: Michael Allen.

Cover design by Dilkash Luhano.

Interior design by Hasnain Aslam.

Printed in the United States of America.

ISBN: 979-8-9990743-0-0

First Edition | 2025

Table of Content

Introduction

Welcome to Entrepreneurial Mindset: Mastering the Mental Game of Business Success. This book isn't about quick hacks, overnight success, or get-rich-quick schemes. It's about something far more powerful, and far more permanent: the way you think.

If you've picked up this book, chances are you've already felt that tug. Maybe you've started a business or are dreaming about one. Maybe you've had some wins and more than a few losses. Or maybe you're just tired of watching others succeed while you feel stuck, frustrated, or uncertain. I've been there. I know what it's like to have ambition burning inside you and doubts whispering just as loudly. That's where mindset comes in.

Entrepreneurship is a mental game before it's anything else. It's not just about spreadsheets, funding rounds, or social media strategy. It's about how you respond to fear. How you bounce back from failure. How you handle success without losing your soul. How you think when no one's watching, and how you act when the pressure is on.

I didn't grow up with money, connections, or a roadmap. I grew up with grit. I've been broke. I've been fired. I've had a truck repossessed. I've juggled parenting, marriages, businesses, and school all at the same time. Through it all, one truth has become clear to me: your mindset determines your altitude. Not your background. Not your resume. Your mindset.

This book is built around the real, raw journey of entrepreneurship. I'll share the science behind personal growth, resilience, confidence, and belief. But I'll also share my story, mistakes and all, because I want you to see what's possible. If a kid from Loris, South Carolina can go from digging in a scrapyard to building successful companies and teaching college courses, then there's no reason you can't build the life and business you want.

Each chapter is focused on a key mental shift or skill you'll need to master. I won't sugarcoat it, entrepreneurship is hard. It'll test you. But it'll also grow you. You'll learn to face your fears, push through setbacks, manage your energy, and believe in yourself in ways you never thought possible.

This book is for dreamers and doers. For people who've failed and want to try again. For those who know deep down they're capable of more, and are finally ready to go get it.

Read with an open heart and a hungry mind. Take notes. Reflect. Apply. This isn't just a book, it's a blueprint.

About the Author

My name is Michael Allen. I'm an entrepreneur, a teacher, a veteran, a husband, a father, and someone who has learned just as much from failure as from success.

I didn't come from money. I didn't have a fast track to the top. I grew up in South Carolina, raised by a single mother who worked multiple jobs to keep food on the table and shoes on my feet. My biological father passed away when I was two. From a young age, I witnessed struggle, but I also witnessed grit. I saw sacrifice. I saw unconditional love. And those early experiences planted the seeds of the mindset that would carry me through life.

When I was ten, my mom married Danny Allen. Danny wasn't just a stepfather, he became my dad. He brought a sense of stability to our lives, and through his leadership and hard work, he introduced me to a world I hadn't seen before. Danny ran a family scrapyard business, and through him, I got my first taste of real work, responsibility, and eventually, business.

At seventeen, I became a father myself. With no clear direction and no resources, I joined the U.S. Army. It offered structure, stability, and an education. I took full advantage, eventually earning an MBA from Coastal Carolina University and later becoming an adjunct business professor, something the younger me would've never thought possible.

But it wasn't academics or military discipline alone that shaped me. It was the scrapyard. Long days, heavy machinery, and harder lessons. That's where I got my real business education: by doing, failing, adapting, and getting back up. I helped run the day-to-day operations and, through that work, co-founded Asbestos Solutions, LLC, my first experience with ownership. That business didn't last due to internal conflicts, but it gave me something priceless: the belief that I could do this. That I was capable of running a company.

That belief changed everything. Today, I run multiple successful businesses. But none of it came easy. I've experienced failed ventures, broken partnerships, and more than one hard reset. I've faced burnout and rebuilt. Through it all, one truth has held: success is 90% mindset, 10% mechanics. Once I shifted how I thought, everything else began to shift too.

I'm not here to preach or pose. I'm here to tell the truth, to share what I've lived, in the hope that it helps you find clarity, confidence, and courage for your own journey. If I can help you avoid even one of the mistakes I've made, then writing this book was worth it.

Chapter 1: The Power of Mindset

If I could only give one tool to every entrepreneur, it wouldn't be money, a mentor, or a business plan. It would be the correct mindset.

Because mindset isn't just one part of the equation, it's the foundation that everything else is built on. It's the lens through which you view challenges, the compass that directs your decisions, and the engine that powers your persistence. It affects how you interpret feedback, how you rebound from setbacks, and how boldly you chase opportunity. Mindset is the filter through which you see every opportunity, every problem, every success, and every failure. It determines what you pursue, how long you pursue it, and what you believe you're capable of along the way.

Your mindset isn't just part of the journey, it is the journey.

I've lived this firsthand. I've had seasons in business where I felt like I couldn't lose, every phone call was a win, every decision opened a new door, and confidence came easy. But I've also had seasons where it felt like I was drowning. When nothing was working, when doubt crept in at every turn, when it took everything I had just to get out of bed and face the day. I've been on both ends of that spectrum, winning with momentum and crawling through resistance.

And here's what I can tell you without hesitation: the difference between those two extremes wasn't what was happening around me. It was what was happening inside me.

My mindset was the variable. It was the difference-maker. It wasn't about resources, it was about resourcefulness. It wasn't about perfect conditions, it was about how I chose to respond to the imperfect ones.

You can have the best strategy in the world, the perfect market, the ideal product, but if your mindset is weak, you'll sabotage yourself before the world ever gets a chance to.

But with the right mindset? You can walk into uncertainty with courage. You can see setbacks as setups. You can keep moving when others quit. You can build something from nothing, not because you had it all figured out, but because you refused to give up.

That's what this chapter, and this book, is about.

Not giving you hype. But helping you build the mental muscles that will carry you through the grind, the growth, and the greatness ahead.

Belief Shapes Behavior

Science backs this up. One of the most fascinating examples is the placebo effect. In countless clinical studies, patients given nothing more than sugar pills, completely inactive substances, report genuine improvements in their symptoms. Why? Because they believe they're being treated. Their brains and bodies respond to the expectation of healing, not the actual chemical content of the pill. That belief triggers a biological chain reaction. Hormones shift. Pain lessens. Recovery accelerates. All because the mind sent the body a different signal.

Belief doesn't just influence behavior, it influences biology. And this isn't limited to medicine. Athletes who visualize performance improvements often experience real gains in skill and focus. Students who believe they're capable of learning retain more. Leaders who believe they can influence change show up more boldly and create more momentum.

I experienced something like this in a less scientific, but no less real, way when I was a kid. I remember faking sick to get out of going to school. I'd lie in bed, pretending I had a fever, a stomachache, whatever it took. But the strange thing was, after a little while, I would actually start to feel sick. My energy would drop. My stomach would tighten. I didn't understand it back then, but now I know what I was experiencing. My body was reacting to the signals I was sending it. I had convinced myself something was wrong, and so my body went along with the story.

That was my first unintentional lesson in how deeply belief can shape reality.

The stories you tell yourself, about who you are, what you're capable of, and what you deserve, don't stay in your head. They manifest in your actions. They bleed into your body language, your tone, your habits. They determine whether you step forward or hold back. Whether you pursue opportunity or talk yourself out of it.

And here's the key: the brain doesn't just react to what's true. It reacts to what it believes is true.

That's why mindset matters. Because the stories you believe shape the life you build.

Case Study:
Thomas Edison and the Lightbulb

Few stories illustrate the power of mindset more clearly than that of Thomas Edison. When working to invent the electric lightbulb, Edison didn't fail a dozen times or even a hundred. He failed over 1,000 times.

In today's world, that many setbacks would be seen as a sign to quit. Investors would pull out. Headlines would mock the effort. Most people would label it as a lost cause.

But Edison saw it differently.

When a reporter once asked him how it felt to fail 1,000 times, Edison famously replied, "I didn't fail 1,000 times. The lightbulb was an invention with 1,000 steps."

That response is pure mindset.
He didn't see failure as defeat. He saw it as data. He didn't take setbacks personally. He treated them like puzzle pieces. His belief never wavered, not because he had proof it would work, but because he was committed to the process long enough to discover how it could work.

Edison's story isn't just about innovation. It's about identity. He believed he was a problem solver, so he kept solving. He believed he was capable, so he kept showing up.

The mindset came first. The invention came later.

And that's the reminder for every entrepreneur: it's not the results that shape your mindset, it's your mindset that shapes the results.

The Mistaken SAT Score

There's a story I love that perfectly illustrates the power of belief. It's about a high school student who was struggling, low grades, inconsistent behavior, and not much encouragement from anyone around him. Teachers had given up on him. He didn't think much of himself either. But then he took the SAT, and when the results came back, he had scored a 1480 out of 1600. That's Ivy League territory. Life-changing.

He was shocked. So was everyone else. But instead of questioning it, he thought, *Maybe I'm smarter than I realized. Maybe I've got what it takes.*

That one piece of information flipped a mental switch. He started to apply himself. He studied harder. Paid attention in class. Changed his friend group. Changed his habits. And most importantly, changed his self-image. The kid who once felt like a failure started acting like someone who was going somewhere.

Fast forward a few years, he graduates high school, goes to college, builds a successful career, and becomes someone most people would look up to.

But here's the twist: years later, he gets a letter from the SAT board. There had been a mistake. His real score wasn't 1480. It was significantly lower. He was one of a small batch of students who had been sent the wrong score due to a processing error.

But by then, it didn't matter.

Because the moment he believed he was capable, he started acting like it. That one score, right or wrong, had rewritten the narrative in his mind. It gave him a new identity to live up to, and he rose to meet it.

That's the power of belief.

It's not about the data. It's about the meaning you attach to it. Belief doesn't wait for evidence, it creates it. Your actions follow your assumptions. And once you start believing that you're capable, that belief starts stacking wins.

Not because something outside of you changed, but because something inside of you did.

Locus of Control: Who's Really in Charge?

Psychologists have a term, **locus of control**, that defines how people perceive the forces that shape their lives. It's not just academic theory. It's a lens that colors every decision, every reaction, every belief about what's possible. And as an entrepreneur, your lens will either limit you or launch you.

Here's the breakdown.

People with an **external locus of control** believe that life happens to them. They blame the economy. They blame their upbringing. They blame the algorithm. When something goes wrong, it's always someone else's fault. When something goes right, they chalk it up to luck. They're passengers in their own story, waiting, hoping, wishing.

Then there are those with an **internal locus of control**. These people believe that, while they can't control every event, they can control their response. They believe in cause and effect. In ownership. In the power of decision-making. Life doesn't happen to them. They happen to life.

This mindset shift is absolutely critical in business. You can't control inflation. You can't control supply chains, pandemics, or whether a big client suddenly pulls out. But you can control your preparation. You can control your pivot. You can control how quickly you adapt, how well you lead, and how much you learn from every setback.

In my own journey, this mindset has been a game-changer. There were times when the market shifted overnight. I could've panicked. I could've played the victim. Instead, I asked, "What's within my control?" And then I got to work. That question, what can I control right now?, has pulled me through more challenges than I can count.

And here's the kicker: when you consistently operate from an internal locus of control, people notice. Investors trust you more. Teams follow you more confidently. Clients feel your stability. Because people naturally gravitate to leaders who don't flinch when things go sideways.

Owning your outcomes doesn't mean blaming yourself for everything. It means believing that you have agency, that your effort, your decisions, and your resilience matter. That you're not a victim of circumstance, you're a creator of outcomes.

Once you adopt that belief, everything changes. You stop waiting. You start building. You stop pointing fingers. You start taking steps.

That's where real power lives, not in controlling the world, but in mastering your mindset.

Final Thought: What You Believe Becomes Who You Become

Your mindset doesn't just influence your decisions, it defines your direction. It shapes your identity, and that identity quietly dictates how you show up every single day. Before the strategy, before the product, before the pitch, there's a belief. And that belief is the root of everything that follows.

Your **mindset shapes your identity.** If you see yourself as a builder, you'll find ways to build. If you believe you're a leader, you'll step into hard conversations. If you identify as someone who figures things out, you'll lean into challenges instead of running from them.

That identity then **shapes your behavior**. It affects what risks you take, what opportunities you pursue, and how you respond when life hits back. It's the internal script playing quietly in the background of every action you take.

And over time, that behavior **shapes your outcomes**. Not overnight. Not magically. But steadily, day by day. Success isn't an accident, it's a byproduct of alignment between belief and behavior.

So ask yourself the hard questions:

- **What do I believe about myself?** Am I someone who finishes what I start? Someone who leads with courage? Someone who adds value wherever I go?

- **What do I believe about success?** Do I see it as a zero-sum game, or as something abundant and available? Do I believe it's reserved for the lucky, or accessible to the disciplined?

- **What do I believe is possible for my future?** Am I playing not to lose, or playing to win? Am I building a job, or building a legacy?

Because here's the truth: the answers to those questions are already shaping your life. Whether you realize it or not, they are the invisible lines on the blueprint of your future.

And the good news? You get to rewrite them. You get to upgrade the script. You get to believe differently, and live differently as a result.

Your next chapter isn't waiting on more time, more money, or more talent. It's waiting on a deeper belief.

Because what you believe becomes who you become.

So choose wisely.

Chapter 2: Overcoming Fear and Embracing Failure

Fear is part of the job description. If you're going to be an entrepreneur, you're going to be afraid. That's not a flaw, it's a feature. Fear means you're pushing boundaries. It means you're stepping into new territory, stretching your capacity, and taking risks that actually matter. It's a signal that you're operating outside your comfort zone, and that's exactly where growth happens.

But here's the key: fear doesn't have to control you. It doesn't have to paralyze you, keep you small, or dictate your decisions. Fear will always show up, but it doesn't have to sit in the driver's seat.

The most successful entrepreneurs aren't fearless, they're just familiar with fear. They've learned how to live with it, how to move with it, and most importantly, how to act in spite of it. They understand that fear and progress are often traveling companions.

They also understand this: failure isn't the enemy. In fact, failure is one of the best teachers you'll ever have, if you're willing to listen. Every failed pitch, every botched launch, every partnership that didn't work out carries a lesson. A blueprint. A warning. A new perspective.

That's what this chapter is about, reframing your relationship with fear and failure so they don't hold you back, but instead help launch you forward. Because if you can learn to walk through fear and learn from failure, you can handle anything this journey throws your way.

What Fear Really Is

Fear isn't just a feeling, it's a biological response. It's your brain doing exactly what it was designed to do: protect you. From the earliest days of human existence, fear kept us alive. It told us to run from predators, to avoid cliffs, to stay close to shelter and safety. That wiring hasn't changed. Your brain still treats any perceived threat, physical, emotional, or financial, as something dangerous. And it triggers the same fight-or-flight response, flooding your body with cortisol, speeding up your heart rate, narrowing your focus.

That's helpful if a bear's chasing you. But when you're trying to pitch a new idea, launch a product, make a big investment, or step into leadership? That same fear can become a cage. It convinces you that the unknown is unsafe, that discomfort equals danger, that risk should be avoided at all costs.

But most entrepreneurial fear isn't about life or death. It's about uncertainty. The fear of looking stupid. The fear of wasting time. The fear of being judged. The fear of losing what you've worked so hard for. And underneath all of it? The fear that maybe you're not enough.

Here's what most people miss: fear isn't the enemy. It's information. It's a signal that you're stepping into unfamiliar territory, stretching, growing, reaching for something bigger. In that way, fear is actually a compass. It tells you where the edge is. Where the resistance lives. And where the breakthrough might be hiding.

It's not there to stop you, it's there to test you. To ask, "How bad do you want it?" To push you to build courage, clarity, and conviction. Because once you stop running from fear and start leaning into it, you realize something powerful:

Fear doesn't mean something's wrong.

It usually means you're about to do something that matters.

My First Real Business Risk

I remember one of the first times I had to make a real entrepreneurial leap. I had been working in the family scrap metal business, learning the ropes, getting my hands dirty, figuring out how the world of business really worked one forklift load at a time. It was gritty, loud, chaotic, and real. That experience gave me a foundation. But then came the moment that changed everything.

My dad, Danny, pulled me aside one day and laid out the idea: we had an opportunity to help start an asbestos abatement company. The market was there. The margins were strong. The team was forming. And he wanted me in.

Now, I didn't negotiate terms or draw up contracts. I wasn't the one putting the deal together. I was young, green, and mostly along for the ride. But what I didn't have in experience, I made up for in willingness. When my dad said, "You're in," I said yes, even though I was nervous.

Looking back, I didn't fully understand what the business even did. I didn't know how complex the work would be, or how serious the regulations were. I didn't know how partnerships could turn sour. I didn't know how hard it would be to balance ownership with learning on the fly. But I said yes anyway. And that yes taught me more than any book or classroom ever could.

It taught me that fear doesn't disappear with more information. It fades with movement. The moment you say, "Let's go," something shifts. You stop analyzing and start becoming. You stop asking, "What if I fail?" and start discovering what happens when you try.

That first leap didn't end with a massive exit or a fairy tale ending. The business eventually closed due to internal conflict. But it gave me something far more valuable than a paycheck or a title, it gave me belief. It made me realize that I could be a part of building something real. That I could take risks, get my hands dirty, figure things out, and still come out standing.

That experience was my initiation into the real world of entrepreneurship. Not the sanitized version. Not the Instagram version. The version where fear is normal, but so is progress.
And the biggest thing I learned?

Action is the antidote to fear.

Redefining Failure

Most people treat failure like it's the end of the road. Like it says something permanent about who they are. But failure isn't final unless you quit. And it isn't personal unless you make it so.

The truth? Failure is a feature of growth, not a bug. It's how you learn what doesn't work so you can figure out what does. It's not a stop sign, it's a data point.

I've never had a failure that didn't teach me something. Some taught me what kind of people not to go into business with. Others taught me how important timing, cash flow, and contracts really are. And more than once, failure has reminded me that my instincts aren't always right, and that's okay, because instinct can be refined.

Failure sharpens you.

Look at James Dyson. Over 5,000 failed prototypes. Five. Thousand. That's not failure. That's testing. That's refining. That's staying in the game long enough to figure it out. Most people would've quit after five tries, or fifty. But he kept going. And now? His name is on one of the most successful product lines in the world.

Walt Disney got fired from a newspaper for "lacking imagination." Imagine that. Then he got turned down by dozens of banks when he pitched Disneyland. They thought it was too risky. Too expensive. Too big. But Walt didn't see failure, he saw resistance. And he kept pushing.

Howard Schultz was told no more than 240 times before someone finally invested in Starbucks. He believed in the vision so much that he kept showing up, even when the world said no. And eventually, one yes changed everything.

The pattern is clear. These weren't superhumans. They were regular people with an extraordinary relationship to failure.

They didn't run from it. They respected it. They studied it. And most importantly, they didn't let it define them.

I've had businesses that didn't work. I've had partnerships that fell apart. I've lost money. Made bad hires. Launched too soon. Waited too long. But none of those moments broke me.

Why?

Because I decided early on that failure wasn't a dead end. It was a detour. A recalibration. A tuition payment to the school of experience.

If you're afraid of failure, that's okay. Most people are. But if you let that fear keep you from starting, from risking, from trying, that's the real failure.

Redefining failure means asking better questions:

- What did I learn?

- What can I apply next time?

- Who did I become in the process?

That shift in perspective doesn't just protect your confidence, it multiplies your progress.

Because once you stop fearing failure, there's nothing left to hold you back.

Learning to Say No

One of the most difficult, and most important, skills I've had to develop as an entrepreneur is the ability to say no.

No to the wrong clients. No to poor fit hires. No to projects that pull you away from your vision. No to distractions, drama, and detours. No to anything that costs more than it's worth.

Saying no isn't just about boundaries, it's about identity. It's about knowing who you are, what you stand for, and what kind of business you're building.

But I'll be honest with you: early on, I was terrible at it.

I wanted to be liked. I wanted to prove myself. I wanted to show I could make it work. So I said yes, to everything.

Yes to clients I knew were a nightmare from the first meeting. Yes to "custom" projects that didn't align with my core services. Yes to employees who didn't show up on time, didn't care about the mission, and drained the energy from the rest of the team. Yes to favors, freebies, discounts, and extra work I didn't have time for.

And guess what? Every one of those yeses came back to bite me.

I told myself I was being generous. Accommodating. Flexible.

But what I was really being? Fearful.

Fearful of confrontation. Fearful of disappointing people. Fearful of conflict. Fearful of being judged.

But here's the hard truth I had to learn: every time you say yes to something that doesn't align, you're saying no to something that does.

You're saying no to your real priorities. No to your real goals. No to the people who are the right fit. No to the future you're trying to build.

And that's not generosity. That's self-sabotage.

The turning point for me came when I realized that the short-term discomfort of saying no was nothing compared to the long-term damage of saying yes to the wrong things.
I remember one client in particular, big name, big opportunity, big headaches. From day one, they were disrespectful, disorganized, and demanding. But I ignored the red flags. I thought, "This will look good on our portfolio. We'll figure it out."

We didn't.

The relationship was a disaster. We lost money, lost time, and lost morale. And when it finally ended, I thought to myself: "I knew better."

That's when I started honoring my gut.

Now? I say no quickly, kindly, and clearly. If it's not a heck yeah, it's a no. If someone's not aligned with our culture or values, they're not on the team. If a deal looks good on paper but feels wrong in my spirit, I walk away.

Not because I'm above it. But because I've learned that protecting your energy, your team, and your vision matters more than padding your numbers.

It's not easy. Saying no will ruffle feathers. You'll disappoint some people. But the right people? They'll respect you more for it.

And the best part? Every time you say no to something that's wrong, you make room for something that's right.

That's what leadership is. Not just making the popular choice, but making the right one.

And sometimes, that starts with one simple word: no.

Tools to Face Fear

Let's get one thing clear: you don't need to eliminate fear. That's not the goal. You need to manage it. Understand it. Channel it. And most importantly, move through it.

Fear is a signal, not a stop sign. It's your body's way of saying, "Pay attention." So listen, but don't let it take the wheel.

Here's how you do that:

1. Reframe It

Fear often shows up as a question: *"What if I fail?"*
But what if you flipped that question?

"What if I learn something I needed to know?"
"What if this actually works?"
"What if this is the breakthrough I've been waiting for?"

The questions you ask yourself determine the answers you find. If you keep asking fear-based questions, you'll keep getting fear-based answers. But when you reframe your fear as opportunity, you stop seeing it as something to run from, and start seeing it as something to run toward.

2. Break It Down

Big fears lose power when you slice them into small steps.

Don't worry about landing the huge client, just reach out to one person today. Don't panic about public speaking, just start by practicing a five-minute talk in front of a friend. Don't obsess over launching a six-figure business, just make your first sale.

When you break fear into bite-sized action, it stops being paralyzing. It starts being manageable. And each little win builds the confidence to take the next step.

3. Visualize Success

I do this all the time. Before a big meeting, a sales pitch, or a difficult conversation, I mentally walk through it. I see myself calm, confident, clear. I picture the handshake. The smile. The outcome I want.

Why? Because your brain doesn't know the difference between something vividly imagined and something actually experienced. Visualization creates familiarity. And familiarity kills fear.

Think of it like pre-rehearsing your future success. So when the moment comes, your mind says, "I've been here before."

4. Ask: What's the Worst That Can Happen?

Seriously. Write it down. Say it out loud. Most of the time, the worst-case scenario isn't nearly as catastrophic as we imagine.

You might lose a little money. You might feel embarrassed. You might get a "no."

Okay, and then what?

You adjust. You recover. You try again. You grow.

But if you let fear keep you frozen, you risk something far worse than failure: regret.

And regret doesn't teach, it lingers.

5. Lean Into Community

Fear grows in silence. It feeds on isolation. But the second you speak it out loud to someone you trust, it starts to shrink.

Find people who get it, mentors, peers, coaches, friends. People who've been where you are and are willing to tell you the truth with love. Talk about the fear. Ask for perspective. Let someone remind you who you are when you forget.

I can't tell you how many times I've shared something I was scared to do, only to have someone say, "That's nothing. I did that last year. Here's how." And just like that, the monster in my head turns back into a manageable challenge. You don't need to be fearless to win. You just need to be faithful to the process. Courage isn't the absence of fear, it's choosing to act anyway.

And with the right tools, the right mindset, and the right people, you can face anything.

Case Study:
Elon Musk and SpaceX

If anyone knows what it means to face fear and push through, it's Elon Musk. Love him or hate him, the man has nerves of steel, and the track record to prove it.

When Musk launched SpaceX, he wasn't some starry-eyed dreamer with unlimited resources. He was a calculated risk-taker betting everything on a vision that most people thought was insane: to build a private company that could launch rockets into space. At the time, space was the domain of governments, NASA, Roscosmos. Billion-dollar budgets. Massive bureaucracies. The idea that a private company could do it better? Laughable.

But Musk believed. And he didn't just invest a little, he poured in over $100 million of his own money. That's not venture capital. That's personal.

Then came the setbacks.
The first rocket launch? Exploded.
Second launch? Failure.
Third launch? Another failure.

Three strikes. And in the world of aerospace, each one cost millions and shattered timelines. At that point, most people would've cut their losses, licked their wounds, and quietly walked away.

But not Musk.

With barely enough money left for one more attempt, he doubled down. That fourth launch? It succeeded.

It didn't just succeed, it changed the game. SpaceX secured a $1.6 billion contract with NASA and proved, for the first time, that private enterprise could send rockets into orbit and bring them back safely. It was a turning point not just for Musk, but for the entire aerospace industry.

Here's what's powerful: Musk wasn't fearless. He was almost broke. He was criticized, ridiculed, and written off. But he had a mindset that refused to back down. He understood a principle that every entrepreneur must learn:

Fear is normal. Setbacks are expected. But belief backed by bold action? That's where breakthroughs are born.

Musk's story isn't just about rockets. It's about resilience. It's about what happens when someone believes in a mission so deeply that failure stops being a reason to quit, and becomes a reason to push harder.

That's the mindset you need. Not just to win, but to keep showing up until the win comes.

Case Study:
Sara Blakely and Spanx

Sara Blakely didn't start with venture capital, a business degree, or industry connections. She started with a pair of scissors, a brilliant idea, and $5,000 in savings. Working by day selling fax machines door-to-door, she spent her nights sketching, researching, and building what would become one of the most disruptive apparel brands of the 21st century.

Her idea? Cut the feet off of control-top pantyhose to create smoother lines under white pants. It was a simple concept, but solving a real problem is often the birthplace of billion-dollar solutions. Blakely wasn't a fashion designer. She wasn't even in the apparel industry. But she had the one thing that separates successful entrepreneurs from sidelined dreamers: conviction.

And she needed it.

Blakely was rejected again and again, by manufacturers who didn't take her seriously, by stores that wouldn't carry her product, and by investors who thought shapewear was a joke. She got laughed out of rooms. She was told "no" so many times that anyone else might've folded. But she kept going.

One of the things that set Blakely apart was the way she viewed failure. She credits much of her mindset to her father, who had a dinner table tradition that most parents would never consider. Every night, he'd ask, "What did you fail at today?" If she didn't have something to report, he'd be disappointed.

Why?

Because in their house, failure wasn't something to be feared, it was proof you were trying. That belief flipped the fear script. Instead of avoiding failure, she pursued action. Instead of aiming for perfection, she aimed for growth.

That mindset became the foundation of Spanx.

Eventually, she got a break. A manufacturer agreed to take a chance. A Neiman Marcus buyer tried the product and placed a small order. Oprah named Spanx one of her favorite things, and the rocket launched.

Today, Spanx is a billion-dollar brand. Sara Blakely became the youngest self-made female billionaire, and later gave back in ways just as bold, like gifting each of her employees $10,000 and two first-class plane tickets anywhere in the world when she sold a majority stake in the company.

Blakely's story is a masterclass in the entrepreneurial mindset. She didn't let rejection define her. She didn't let fear freeze her. And she didn't wait to be qualified, she started, stayed scrappy, and learned along the way.

The takeaway? Failure is not the opposite of success, it's the path to it.

My Reminder to You

You're going to be scared. That's okay. Fear doesn't mean you're weak. It means you're stretching. It means you're stepping outside your comfort zone, into the arena where growth actually happens. Every entrepreneur, leader, and visionary you admire has felt the same fear you're feeling now. The difference? They didn't stop.

You're going to make mistakes. That's part of it. Mistakes don't mean you're broken or unqualified, they mean you're moving. You're trying. You're testing, experimenting, pushing into unknown territory. Mistakes are data. They're your teachers. Embrace them. Study them. Then course-correct and move forward stronger.

You're going to fail. That's how you learn. There will be days when the deal falls through, when the client walks away, when your best idea flops. Don't confuse those moments with your identity. Failure is an event, not a person. Let it refine you, not define you.

But if you're willing to face the fear and move forward anyway, you're going to win. Maybe not immediately. Maybe not exactly the way you imagined. But over time, your courage will compound. Your grit will pay off. Your resilience will open doors you never could've kicked down with confidence alone.

Because here's the truth: the most dangerous thing you can do as an entrepreneur is let fear make your decisions. Fear will keep you small. Fear will keep you safe. And fear will keep you from the life, business, and legacy you were born to build.

So when it shows up, and it will, look it in the eye and say, "You don't get to drive today, fear, I've got the wheel and we are going places!"

Chapter 3: Developing Resilience

In entrepreneurship, it's not a matter of if you'll get knocked down, it's when. The market shifts. A deal collapses. A trusted team member quits. A product flops. Something breaks, sometimes everything at once. And when that moment comes, it won't be your intelligence, your degrees, or your Instagram following that carries you forward.

It will be your resilience.

Resilience is the ability to recover. To take a punch and keep moving. To absorb the hits without losing the will to swing back. It's not about bouncing back to who you were, it's about bouncing forward into who you're becoming. It's not about perfection. It's about persistence. Grit. Staying in the fight when others would tap out.

I've needed resilience more times than I care to count. And not just in business. I've faced personal losses, financial setbacks, moments where I questioned everything, from my strategies to my sanity. I've had seasons where the pressure was so intense it felt like my chest would crack under the weight of it all. But every time I stood back up, bloodied, wiser, more focused, I realized something:

Resilience isn't just a trait. It's a skill. And like any skill, it can be developed.

This chapter is about building that skill. It's about learning to take the hits, protect your vision, and keep moving, no matter what life or business throws at you.

Because you can't control the storm. But you can control how you stand in it.

Life Hits First

I didn't grow up with much. My mother worked multiple jobs just to keep the lights on and food on the table. There wasn't a trust fund, a silver spoon, or a safety net. What we lacked in money, we made up for in grit. I watched her stretch every dollar, sacrifice her own needs, and keep going, no matter how tired she was. That kind of example leaves a mark.

I lost my biological father when I was just two years old. I never had the chance to know him. What I did know, from a young age, was loss. And for a while, I had a stepfather whose presence brought more pain than peace, a time I don't often talk about, but one that shaped my understanding of adversity early on.

Then, when I was ten, everything changed. My mom met and married Danny Allen. And from the start, Danny showed up in every way that mattered. He was steady, dependable, and driven. He didn't say a lot, but when he did, you listened. He ran a scrapyard, worked with his hands, managed people, solved problems, and modeled what it meant to lead without a title. Watching him work, watching him lead, was my first real exposure to business, even if I didn't realize it at the time.

I became a father myself before I could legally vote. I didn't have a map. I didn't have a plan. But I had a powerful reason to figure it out. I joined the Army because I needed direction. I needed discipline. I needed a way to take care of my family. And the military gave me all of that, and more.

That was my life before I ever launched a business. Before I pitched my first client. Before I knew what ROI or scaling or systems even meant. Real life hit me first. And that gave me an edge.

Because by the time business threw me a curveball, I'd already taken a few punches. I had some scar tissue. I wasn't shocked by struggle. I expected it.

But here's the thing: resilience isn't something you inherit, it's something you develop. It's not handed to you. It's forged. You build it in the moments when you want to quit, but don't. When you fall down, but choose to stand up anyway.
Resilience is a decision. And I've made it again and again.

What Resilience Really Is

Resilience isn't just about grinding through hardship or toughing it out until the storm passes. It's more nuanced than that. Resilience is about recovery. It's about how you think, how you adapt, and how you respond when life, or business, hits you in the mouth.

It's not just endurance. Endurance is holding your breath and waiting for it to be over. Resilience is learning how to breathe under pressure. It's the ability to bend without breaking, to adjust the plan without abandoning the mission.

True resilience is mental agility. It's being able to shift your thinking in real time when the facts change. It's emotional flexibility, the ability to acknowledge pain without being owned by it. It's learning while you're bleeding and still finding the courage to step back into the ring.

Psychologist Martin Seligman, a pioneer in the field of positive psychology, offers a framework that helped me put words to what I'd already experienced. He identified three mental habits, the "Three P's", that determine how we respond to adversity:

- **Personalization:** Do you blame yourself for everything that goes wrong? When a deal falls through or a project flops, do you immediately think, "This is all my fault," even if it isn't? Resilient people separate the event from their identity. They take responsibility without self-condemnation.

- **Permanence:** Do you believe the pain will last forever? When you lose a client, have a bad quarter, or take a hit, do you catastrophize it into a permanent state? Resilient people remind themselves: "This is a season, not a sentence."

- **Pervasiveness:** Do you let one setback bleed into everything else? A lost sale becomes "I'm bad at business." A tough conversation becomes "I'm a terrible leader." Resilient people compartmentalize. They isolate the problem so it doesn't contaminate their confidence.

When I first came across this concept, it was like someone turned on the lights. I saw how easy it was to let failure become personal, permanent, and pervasive, and how damaging that thinking was.

The strongest entrepreneurs I know have trained themselves to reframe quickly. They don't deny what's hard, but they don't drown in it either. They name the setback, learn from it, and move forward.

They don't let failure write the ending. They use it to shape the next chapter.

My Truck Got Repossessed

I'll never forget the call. The repo guy didn't yell, didn't make threats, didn't even sound aggressive. He was just matter-of-fact. "I'm coming to get the truck," he said. That was it. And deep down, I already knew it was coming. I was behind on payments, stretched too thin, and out of options.

I didn't waste time panicking. I went into salvage mode. Literally.

I took off the brush guard, pulled the toolbox, and swapped the nice rims and tires for a beat-up set I found in the scrapyard. Then I sold the good parts to scrape together every dollar I could. I wasn't trying to be spiteful, I was just trying to survive. That truck was a loss, but I wasn't about to lose more than I had to.

With that money, I bought the only vehicle I could afford: a ragged, old Kia Sephia. It was a straight drive with more problems than personality. The driver's side door wouldn't open from the inside, so I had to roll down the window, reach out, and pop the latch. The passenger side only opened from the inside, which meant I had to do a little gymnastics just to give someone a ride. A few of the windows didn't roll down at all. And cosmetically? It looked like something that should've been recycled into a lawn chair.

But you know what? That car ran. And for almost two years, it carried me to every job site, every meeting, every opportunity. It wasn't pretty. It wasn't powerful. But it was mine, and it moved forward. And that's all I needed.

Driving that car was humbling. At times, it was embarrassing. But looking back? It was one of the most important seasons of my life. Because every time

I fired up that engine, I was reminded: I didn't quit. I didn't fold. I was still in the game.

That's what resilience looks like. It's not always dramatic or glamorous. Sometimes, it's just rolling up your sleeves, finding a workaround, and doing what needs to be done, no matter how it looks from the outside.

Resilience is what you do when the world expects you to crumble, but you drive forward anyway.

Habits That Build Resilience

Resilience isn't some mystical trait you either have or you don't. It's a muscle. And like any muscle, it's built through repetition, intentionality, and discipline. The people who seem "naturally resilient" aren't born that way, they've just developed habits that help them recover faster and push farther. Here are the habits that have worked for me:

1. **Practice Gratitude Under Pressure**
   When life feels heavy, gratitude feels like the last thing on your mind. But that's exactly when you need it most. I make it a point, every morning, to name three things I'm thankful for. Even when I'm facing payroll stress, a tough conversation, or a curveball I didn't see coming, I pause and ask: "What's still good?"
   It doesn't make the stress disappear, but it gives me perspective. Gratitude is a shield. It reminds me that even when I'm struggling, I'm still blessed, and that shift in focus often gives me the fuel to face the day.

2. **Run Toward the Hard Things**
   Avoidance is the enemy of resilience. Every time you dodge a difficult decision or delay a hard conversation, you reinforce fear and weaken your leadership muscles. Resilience grows when you lean in.
   That means sending the invoice even if you're nervous. Having the tough talk with a team member. Calling the client who's upset. Handling the tax issue instead of ignoring the email.
   Avoidance feels easier in the short term, but it costs you energy, clarity, and confidence in the long run.

When you start running toward the hard things, you realize most of them weren't as bad as you imagined. And more importantly, you realize you're stronger than you thought.

3. Strengthen Your Mental Diet

Your brain is like your body: what you feed it determines how it functions. Junk in, junk out.

That's why I'm careful about what I allow into my mind. I read books that challenge me to grow. I listen to podcasts that elevate my thinking. I surround myself with conversations that sharpen me.

I've learned to guard my attention like my future depends on it, because it does.

News cycles, drama-filled social media, complaining coworkers, toxic environments, they all chip away at your resilience if you're not careful. Choose a mental diet that energizes, not drains.

4. Don't Isolate

When things fall apart, most people retreat. They stop answering calls. They ghost their network. They pretend they're okay when they're drowning. I've been tempted to do that too.

But isolation is a trap. It amplifies fear, multiplies anxiety, and disconnects you from the very people who can help you push through.

That's why I've learned to reach out, even when it's uncomfortable. A quick text to a friend. A phone call to a mentor. A vulnerable check-in with someone I trust.

Even prayer. Especially prayer.

You don't need a huge circle, just a strong one. People who will remind you who you are when you forget. People who will tell you the truth and not just what you want to hear.

Whatever you do, don't do this alone.

5. Build a Resilience Routine

Most people track their goals, but I also track my grit.

At the end of each day, I journal what drained me and what fueled me. I note what went well and what didn't. I reflect on what I learned, and where I need to grow.

This isn't just journaling for the sake of it, it's pattern recognition. It helps me see what's working, where I'm slipping, and how to adjust before burnout takes root.

Some days, the entry is a win. Some days, it's a mess. But every entry reminds me: I'm still in motion. I'm still showing up. I'm still building resilience.

Case Study: Viktor Frankl

Viktor Frankl was a Jewish psychiatrist and neurologist who survived four Nazi concentration camps, including Auschwitz. He lost his parents, his brother, and his pregnant wife in the Holocaust. And yet, in the middle of one of the most horrific chapters of human history, he discovered something life-altering: that while we can't always control our circumstances, we can always control our response.

His book, Man's Search for Meaning, is one of the most profound explorations of human resilience ever written. It's not a business book, but every entrepreneur should read it. Frankl wrote from a place of deep suffering and profound insight. He watched men crumble under the weight of hopelessness, and others rise in quiet strength. And he came to this conclusion: it wasn't the strongest who survived. It wasn't the smartest. It was those who found meaning in the midst of their suffering. Those who believed their pain had purpose. Those who chose, again and again, not to surrender their inner life, even when everything else was stripped away.

Frankl noticed that even in the camps, the people who had something to live for, whether it was reuniting with a loved one, completing a manuscript, or simply helping others survive, endured longer and with more dignity. He called this the "last of the human freedoms": the ability to choose one's attitude in any given set of circumstances.

One of his most powerful quotes says it all:
"When we are no longer able to change a situation, we are challenged to change ourselves."

Entrepreneurship doesn't even come close to the horrors Frankl lived through. But the principle he taught, the idea that our response is always within our control, couldn't be more relevant.

When a deal falls apart...
When a client walks away...
When you get blindsided by a market shift...

When everything feels like it's collapsing and you have no playbook for what comes next...

You still have agency. You still have choice. You can still decide who you're going to be in that moment.

That's what Frankl teaches us. That resilience isn't just about survival, it's about meaning. It's about anchoring yourself to something deeper than money, success, or comfort. It's about choosing purpose over panic. Adaptation over despair. Growth over bitterness.

And that mindset? It'll carry you through far more than just a tough quarter or a bad investment. It'll carry you through life.

Final Thought: Bounce Forward

You're going to get hit. Life will shake you. Business will humble you. People will disappoint you. Plans will unravel.

That's not pessimism, it's reality. Entrepreneurship isn't a straight line. It's a roller coaster without a seatbelt, and the only thing keeping you grounded is the strength of your mindset.

But hear me clearly: you are not done.
You are not broken.
You are being forged.

You're not being punished, you're being prepared.

Every challenge you face has the potential to teach you something essential. Every disappointment is a door to new clarity. Every failure is a forge that strengthens your resolve, sharpens your skills, and stretches your capacity to lead.

Think of business like running a marathon blindfolded. You don't know where the finish line is. You don't know how much further you have to go. All you know is that your legs are burning, your breath is short, and everything in you is screaming to quit.

And that's when most people stop.

But what if they were just steps away? What if they gave up ten feet from the breakthrough?

That's the danger of giving in too soon, and the power of pushing forward anyway. Because in this game, the ones who win aren't always the smartest, fastest, or most connected. They're the ones who can endure. The ones who keep showing up. The ones who take the next step, even when they can't see the finish.

Resilience isn't just about bouncing back, it's about bouncing forward. It's not returning to who you were. It's becoming someone stronger. Smarter. Wiser. More grounded. More capable.

So when the storm hits, don't just survive. Grow from it. Let it refine you, not define you. Let the setback become your setup. Let the fall teach you how to rise.

And most importantly, keep running. Even when it's dark. Even when you're tired. Even when you have no idea how close the finish line might be.

Because if you do, you'll reach it. And when you do, you'll realize: every step was worth it.

Chapter 4: Cultivating a Growth Mindset

Every entrepreneur eventually hits a wall. It might come in the form of a failed product launch, a financial setback, a lost customer, or even burnout. It's not a matter of if, it's when. And when that wall shows up, it forces a decision: will you stop, or will you grow?

For some, the wall becomes a dead end. They throw up their hands and say, "I guess I wasn't cut out for this." They shrink back, pivot away, or quit entirely. Not because they weren't capable, but because they believed the wall meant they couldn't go any further.

For others, that same wall becomes a pivot point. A moment of redirection. A signal that it's time to adapt, evolve, and level up. They ask different questions: "What's this trying to teach me?" "What am I not seeing yet?" "How can I use this to get better?"

The difference between those two responses isn't talent, luck, or even timing, it's mindset.

More specifically, it's whether you see that wall as permanent, or as something you can learn to climb over, walk around, or break straight through.

That's the essence of a growth mindset. It's the belief that your skills, intelligence, and capabilities are not fixed, that they can be developed through effort, experience, and persistence. It's the difference between saying "I'm not good at this" and saying "I'm not good at this yet."

A growth mindset doesn't eliminate obstacles. It equips you to face them with curiosity instead of fear. It turns challenges into stepping stones and failures into feedback.

In business, as in life, the people who go the furthest aren't the ones who never fall. They're the ones who believe they can keep growing, no matter what.

What It Means to Grow

A growth mindset is the belief that your abilities are not set in stone. That intelligence, talent, and success are not the exclusive domain of the naturally gifted. Instead, they're cultivated, earned through effort, sharpened by feedback, and expanded through learning.

It's the opposite of the fixed mindset, which tells you that you either have it or you don't. That if you fail, it must mean you're not smart enough. That if something doesn't come easily, it's not for you.

Dr. Carol Dweck, the psychologist who popularized this concept, conducted groundbreaking research with students. She found a striking pattern: those praised for effort developed resilience and confidence, while those praised for intelligence became risk-averse. Why? Because when you're taught to value outcomes over effort, you start avoiding anything that could make you look less than perfect.

But when effort is celebrated, struggle becomes a sign of growth, not inadequacy. A mistake isn't a verdict, it's data. It means you're stretching, challenging yourself, and building capacity.

And this doesn't just apply to kids. As entrepreneurs, we need to unlearn the belief that we should always have the answers. That being good means never messing up. It's a lie that keeps too many people stuck.

Growth mindset reframes the whole game. It says, "I can get better at this." It turns "I can't" into "I haven't... yet." It invites curiosity instead of fear. Progress instead of perfection.

Looking back, I wish I'd fully grasped this earlier in life. I used to equate success with getting it right the first time. Now, I realize the real success is sticking with it long enough to figure it out. It's staying open. Staying teachable. Staying in motion. That's what it really means to grow.

My Growth Mindset Advantage

I've always had this belief, maybe a little naive, maybe a little bold, that I could do anything I truly set my mind to. I didn't always have the answers, the experience, or the resources. But I had this inner voice that said, "You'll figure it out." And more often than not, I did.

That mindset, that core belief, has been one of the greatest assets in my life. It's what gave me the confidence to say yes to new ventures when everything in me was unsure. It's what made me raise my hand in rooms where I was the least experienced. It's what pushed me to keep going when others might have backed down or walked away.

I'm not saying it always worked out. It didn't. I've had my share of flops, ideas that didn't pan out, skills I overestimated, moves I made too soon. There were times I jumped before I was ready and landed flat on my face. But here's the thing: I never believed those moments defined me. I believed they refined me.

That's the real edge a growth mindset gives you. Not immunity from failure, but immunity from being paralyzed by it. When you believe you can grow, you stop seeing failure as evidence that you're not good enough. You start seeing it as part of the curriculum.

And that belief has carried me through some tough seasons. When the money was tight. When the deals fell through. When people doubted me, or when I doubted myself. That quiet, steady belief that I could grow into whatever the moment required kept me in the game.

I've seen entrepreneurs with all the talent in the world give up because they didn't believe they could get better. And I've seen others with average skills rise to incredible heights simply because they refused to quit growing.

So if there's one mindset trait I'd pass on to every entrepreneur reading this, it's this: You don't have to be the best right now. You just have to believe that you can become the best version of yourself, with time, effort, and relentless growth.

Learning Is a Skill

One of the biggest lies we're told, especially in the business world, is that successful people are just "naturals." That they were born with the gift. That they just "get it" without trying. It's a convenient story, because it gives the rest of us an excuse. If they're just built differently, then maybe we're off the hook. Maybe we don't have to risk failing at something new.

But that idea is pure fiction.

The truth is, a growth mindset means recognizing that every skill is learnable. Leadership isn't inherited, it's built. Communication, problem solving, delegation, financial literacy, none of it is magic. It's all just practice, feedback, and persistence over time.

I wasn't born a great leader. I didn't walk into a room and instantly command respect. I learned through trial, error, and observation. I studied people who did it well. I mimicked what worked and scrapped what didn't. I fumbled through hard conversations. I got feedback that stung, but I listened anyway.

I wasn't born with business instincts either. My education came from the field, not the classroom. I learned to read contracts because I signed bad ones. I learned to manage cash flow because I ran out. I learned to hire better because I hired wrong. My knowledge wasn't gifted to me, it was earned with experience, risk, and reflection.

Sales? I improved by embarrassing myself more times than I can count. By mis-reading cues, botching pitches, and watching deals slip through my fingers. Over time, I learned what to say, when to say it, and most importantly, how to listen.

Systems? I learned by burning out. By realizing that working harder wasn't the answer, I needed to work smarter. That meant studying operations, building processes, and letting go of control. All of that took time.

And that's the key: every time I leaned in and committed to learning, I got better. Sometimes slowly. Sometimes painfully. But always forward.

You're not supposed to be brilliant on day one. You're supposed to be curious. Open. Willing to stumble so that you can stand taller next time.

Learning is a skill. And the more you practice it, the faster everything else develops. You don't have to be the smartest in the room, you just have to be the most committed to growth.

Failure Is a Better Teacher Than Success

Failure teaches with a sharper edge than success ever could. It's immediate, it's personal, and it's unforgettable. Success can sometimes cloud your judgment, inflate your ego, or even disguise bad habits. But failure strips everything away. It demands reflection. It demands growth.

I've made choices that hurt. Deals that went sideways. Hires I regretted. Partnerships that turned toxic. Each of those decisions cost me money, time, relationships and sleep. And yeah, some of those moments still sting when I think about them. But I don't regret them. Because every one of those failures taught me something I couldn't have learned from a win.

Failure, when viewed through the lens of growth, stops being a stop sign. It becomes a signal. A lesson. A mirror.

I remember one particular business partnership that fell apart, fast. At the time, I felt betrayed. I had poured my energy into that venture, shared resources, extended trust, and believed we were aligned. But it turned out we weren't even on the same map. Communication broke down. Values clashed. Promises were broken.

At first, I was angry. Disappointed. Embarrassed, even. But once I got some distance from it, I started breaking it down like game film. I looked for what I missed. What signs were there that I ignored? What questions should I have asked early on? Where did I fail to protect myself or set the right boundaries?

And I'll tell you this, I've never repeated those mistakes again.

That experience became my tuition. The cost of that failure became the down payment on wiser decisions, stronger contracts, and better instincts in the future. I learned to trust, but verify. To document everything. To define roles, expectations, and exit strategies clearly from day one.

And more than anything, I learned that failure isn't fatal. It's formative. It shapes you if you let it.

I don't seek failure, but I no longer fear it. Because I know that behind every failure is an education that no classroom can provide. The trick is to extract the lesson without carrying the bitterness.

So don't be afraid to fall. Just don't fall the same way twice. Because in business, your losses can become your leverage, if you're willing to learn.

Case Study: Angela Duckworth and the Power of Grit

Psychologist Angela Duckworth didn't set out to become a bestselling author or a TED sensation. She began her professional journey as a public school teacher in New York City, standing in front of classrooms filled with students from all backgrounds, abilities, and temperaments. What struck her wasn't who was the smartest, it was who stuck with it.

Time and again, she noticed that the students who excelled weren't necessarily the most gifted or naturally talented. They were the ones who showed up early, stayed late, asked questions, and didn't flinch in the face of failure. They weren't always the best, but they were relentless.

That observation led her to leave teaching and pursue a Ph.D. in psychology. Her research eventually culminated in a groundbreaking conclusion: success doesn't correlate most closely with IQ, social intelligence, or even physical health. It correlates with grit.

Grit, as Duckworth defines it, is passion and perseverance toward long-term goals. It's the willingness to endure boredom, frustration, and setbacks in pursuit of something bigger. It's not flashy. It's not instant. But it works.

In her now-famous studies, Duckworth examined cadets at West Point Military Academy. She tracked who made it through their brutal first year, known as "Beast Barracks", and who dropped out. Surprisingly, academic scores and physical fitness weren't the most accurate predictors. It was grit. The cadets who mentally committed to the process, who expected pain and showed up anyway, outlasted those with more "natural" advantages.

She also studied national spelling bee finalists, top corporate leaders, and elite performers in various industries. Again and again, grit outperformed raw ability.

Her book Grit: The Power of Passion and Perseverance became a runaway success, not because it promised hacks or shortcuts, but because it validated what many of us knew deep down: the path to greatness is messy, long, and rarely glamorous. And that's okay.

Grit doesn't mean you never struggle. It means you refuse to let the struggle stop you. It's not just about effort, it's about consistent effort, day after day, year after year, toward a goal that matters.

And here's why this case study matters in the context of growth mindset: grit and growth are teammates. Grit is the muscle, growth is the mindset. One says, "I can improve." The other says, "And I will, no matter how long it takes."

If you want to succeed in business, or in life, you need both. The belief that you can grow, and the determination to keep growing when it gets hard.

Because that's how progress happens: not in leaps, but in grit-fueled steps.

The Power of "Yet"

There's one tiny word that completely changed the way I talk to myself. YET.

"I don't know how to scale this business... yet."
"I haven't figured out how to lead this team... yet."
"I'm not confident in this area... yet."

That one syllable is a game-changer. It shifts the tone from defeat to development. It acknowledges your current limitations without accepting them as permanent. "Yet" adds possibility to what might otherwise sound like failure.

So many people live in mental prisons built by statements like, "I'm not good at sales," "I can't speak in public," or "I'm terrible with numbers." But all of those can become open doors if you simply add yet.

What "yet" does is introduce time into the equation. It implies that with effort, growth, and practice, what is currently out of reach can become second nature. It transforms a fixed mindset into a growth-oriented one.

Think about how this plays out in business. Instead of saying, "I can't hire a team," you say, "I haven't learned how to hire effectively... yet." That subtle shift keeps the window open. It gives your brain permission to look for solutions instead of reasons to quit.

I've used this technique in real time. When things go wrong, when I feel overwhelmed, unqualified, or in over my head, I'll literally stop and say to myself, "Okay, I haven't figured this out... yet." And that pause? It gives me just enough space to breathe, regroup, and start thinking like a problem-solver again.

It's not magic. But it is powerful. Over time, those small rewrites become new mental scripts. And those scripts shape your decisions, your confidence, and your results.

Try it for a week. Catch yourself the next time you make a limiting statement, and tag it with yet. Watch how your outlook shifts. How your energy changes. How your brain starts asking, "Okay, if not yet... then how soon?"

Because sometimes, the difference between stuck and unstoppable is just one word.

Building a Growth Business

A growth mindset doesn't just change you, it transforms your business. The same principles that push an individual forward can and should be baked into the culture of the company they lead. Because at the end of the day, companies don't grow, people do. And when the people inside a business are learning, evolving, and thinking bigger, the business can't help but reflect that growth.

Think about the best companies you know. They aren't rigid. They're curious. They test, iterate, and pivot when necessary. They're not stuck on being right, they're focused on getting it right.

That's what it means to build a growth business.

It starts with leadership. If you, as the founder or CEO, are constantly learning, reading, asking questions, and embracing feedback, that posture filters down to every department. You create an environment where improvement isn't a one-time project, it's a constant priority.

That means:

- **Encouraging your team to bring ideas**,
  even if they're rough drafts. Innovation rarely shows up fully polished. Let people contribute without fear of judgment. The worst thing you can do is punish creativity.

- **Creating feedback loops that improve execution.**
  Whether it's a customer survey, a team debrief, or a simple one-on-one, every piece of feedback is an opportunity to refine and grow.

- **Treating failure as data, not disaster.**
  If something flops, dig into why. What went wrong? What can we learn? What should we tweak next time? Failure is feedback, plain and simple.

- **Prioritizing evolution over ego.**
  This might be the hardest part. As entrepreneurs, we get attached to our ideas. But sometimes, the best thing you can do is kill your darlings, let

go of that service, that process, that product that's no longer serving your mission. Growth demands humility.

- **Challenging the status quo.**
"This is the way we've always done it" is a death sentence for innovation. Ask your team: "If we were starting from scratch today, what would we do differently?" That one question has sparked breakthroughs in my companies more times than I can count.

In a growth business, no one has all the answers, but everyone is committed to finding better ones. You're not building a house of cards, you're building a living, breathing system. One that gets smarter over time, stronger with pressure, and more valuable with age.

So don't just chase growth in revenue. Build it into your culture. Because a growth mindset isn't just a personal advantage, it's a competitive one.

Final Thought: You Are Capable of More

You are not done. You are not stuck. And you are not defined by what you've accomplished so far.

The truth is, most people stop growing not because they've reached their potential, but because they've stopped believing in what's possible. They hit a plateau and think it's the peak. But your current reality isn't the ceiling, it's the foundation. It's just the starting point for what's still ahead.

Your past may explain you, but it does not define you. Your failures, your struggles, your slow starts, they are not life sentences. They are training grounds. They are the rough drafts of your future success.

The limits you feel right now? They aren't permanent. They're just skills you haven't mastered yet. Mindsets you haven't adopted. Tools you haven't picked up. That's all growth is, adding what's missing so you can become who you were meant to be.

The most impressive leaders I know aren't the smartest or the most naturally gifted. They're the ones who stayed hungry. The ones who remained teachable. The ones who never stopped adapting, asking questions, and leaning into the uncomfortable work of change.

That's what a growth mindset is really about. It's not about having it all figured out. It's about being committed to figuring it out. It's not about being fearless, it's about being focused. It's not about staying safe, it's about stepping up.

So if you take nothing else from this chapter, let it be this:

You can become the person your vision requires.

That future version of you, the one who leads with clarity, builds with confidence, and impacts others with purpose, is not a fantasy. It's a byproduct of the choices you make today.

Believe in that version of yourself. Invest in them. Build toward them.

Because once you believe that kind of growth is possible, everything else becomes possible too.

Chapter 5: Positive Thinking and Affirmations

You've probably heard the phrase, "Your thoughts become your reality." At first glance, it can sound like a motivational cliché, something you'd see on a coffee mug or a social media meme. But if you've spent any meaningful time as an entrepreneur, you've seen just how true it really is. Not because positive thinking magically makes things happen, but because your thoughts shape your focus. Your focus drives your actions. And your actions build your outcomes.

That's not just inspiration, that's psychology and performance science. Your mindset sets the tone for everything else. When you think positively, you notice opportunities instead of obstacles. You respond to challenges with creativity instead of panic. You keep moving forward when others freeze or fold.

Positive thinking isn't about pretending problems don't exist. It's not about blind optimism or ignoring facts. It's about choosing your lens. It's about deciding that even when things look messy, uncertain, or even bleak, you still have the power to respond with clarity, hope, and grit.

As an entrepreneur, you will be tested. Your patience, your energy, your confidence, they'll all be stretched thin at some point. In those moments, your mindset becomes either your anchor or your undoing. Positive thinking doesn't guarantee success. But negative thinking almost always guarantees failure, or at least a much harder path to success.

And that's why this chapter matters. Because if you can train your thoughts, you can transform your outcomes. It all starts with how you choose to think when things get hard.

The Mental Loop

Your mind is always talking. Narrating. Judging. Predicting. Planning. Solving problems before they happen, or creating problems that were never really there. It's the constant mental commentary that runs in the background of your life. And whether you realize it or not, that voice is shaping how you show up.

For a lot of people, that inner voice is soaked in fear, doubt, and self-criticism. It whispers, "You're not ready," or "This will never work." But for me, the danger has always been the opposite: overconfidence.

I've always believed I could figure things out, even when I had no experience, no plan, and no backup. That belief has fueled a lot of bold decisions in my life. It's helped me launch businesses, chase opportunities, and rebound from failure. It's one of the reasons I've succeeded.

But here's the thing about unchecked confidence: it can become arrogance. It can blind you. I've rushed into deals without doing enough due diligence. I've taken on more than I could handle because I assumed I'd "make it work." I've ignored wise counsel because I didn't want to hear anything that sounded like hesitation.

Sometimes, you don't need to be more confident, you need to be more aware. That's why I've learned to create space between the thought and the action. I pause and check in with myself. I ask:

- Am I moving fast because it's right, or because I'm afraid to wait?
- Am I trusting my gut, or resisting hard truths?
- Is this boldness, or is it bravado?

That self-awareness has made a huge difference. It hasn't made me slower, it's made me sharper. I still trust my instincts, but I also trust reflection. I still move fast, but I move with clarity.

Mindset isn't just about believing in yourself. It's about managing the narrative in your head so it doesn't run the show unchecked. When you master that loop, when you become the author of your thoughts instead of just the audience, you start to operate at a whole new level.

The Broaden-and-Build Theory

Psychologist Barbara Fredrickson developed what she called the "Broaden-and-Build" theory, a game-changer for understanding how emotions impact performance, especially in high-stakes environments like entrepreneurship.

Her research revealed that positive emotions do more than just make us feel good in the moment. They actually expand our cognitive capacity. They help us take in more information, see more creative solutions, build stronger relationships, and access parts of our brain that are otherwise locked down when we're stressed or afraid.

Think of it like this: when you're in a negative emotional state, anxious, angry, overwhelmed, your mind goes into tunnel vision. Your brain is wired for survival, so it focuses on the immediate threat. It closes off options. It's not thinking long-term or creatively. It's thinking, "How do I get through the next five minutes?"

But when you're in a positive emotional state, grateful, joyful, hopeful, your brain opens up. You start to see new angles. You become more resourceful. You collaborate better. You learn faster. You're not just reacting, you're creating.

In business, that kind of mental expansion is everything.

Entrepreneurs live in a world of problems: market shifts, customer issues, cash flow crunches. If your mindset is stuck in scarcity or fear, you'll only ever see the obstacles. But if you practice positivity, not blind optimism, but intentional, grounded positivity, you open yourself up to see the opportunities hiding in plain sight.

That's the edge. That's why positive thinking isn't fluff, it's fuel.

Fredrickson's work proves that the more you cultivate positive emotions, the more you build resilience, adaptability, and creative problem-solving. You quite literally broaden your mindset and build better outcomes.

So yes, a positive attitude might help you feel better. But more importantly, it helps you lead better, think better, and build better.

My Commitment to Positivity

Positivity has always come naturally to me. I've always been the guy who believes things will work out, who sees opportunity in the middle of chaos, who laughs when others would panic. It's not a gimmick. It's how I'm wired. I genuinely believe that, given enough time and effort, problems get solved and better days show up.

But even with that wiring, I've come to understand that positivity isn't something you're born with, it's something you have to protect, nurture, and practice intentionally. Life will test it. Business will pressure it. The world won't hand you joy, you have to choose it, again and again.

I've had seasons where the weight of everything nearly wore me down. Teams underperforming, cash flow dipping, family stress stacking up, and the future feeling foggy. It would've been easy to spiral into frustration, blame, or even apathy. But I learned early on that negativity doesn't solve problems, it just makes them heavier.

So I made a conscious decision: to stay grounded in gratitude, no matter what was happening around me. I started by controlling my inputs. I stopped feeding on negativity, cut back the noise, turned off the voices that only stirred up fear or drama, and replaced them with voices that built me up.

I became ruthless about guarding my thoughts. If something didn't serve my peace, my clarity, or my mission, it didn't get space in my mind. That meant choosing my conversations more carefully, limiting complaints, and redirecting worry into action.

I made positivity a practice, not a personality trait. I wrote down what I was grateful for. I celebrated small wins. I trained my brain to focus on solutions, not just problems. And that choice made me a better leader. A more grounded decision-maker. A more attractive force in the marketplace.

Because here's what I've learned: people are drawn to hope. To strength. To light. Positivity isn't just good for your mental health, it's magnetic. It draws the right clients, the right team members, the right partners.

Staying positive didn't mean pretending everything was perfect. It meant refusing to let the imperfections define the whole picture. It meant leading with vision, even when the path wasn't clear.

And that's what kept my businesses moving forward, an unshakable belief that something better was always on the horizon, as long as I stayed focused, faithful, and forward-facing.

Affirmations: Speaking Your Future

Affirmations aren't about wishful thinking, they're about intentional programming. They are short, deliberate statements that help shape your identity, direct your behavior, and build your belief system. The words you say to yourself, especially when repeated consistently, have the power to rewire your mind and reshape your reality.

Here's why they work: your subconscious doesn't judge. It doesn't question whether something is true or false, it simply absorbs whatever it hears most often. That's why negative self-talk is so dangerous. If you constantly tell yourself things like, "I always mess up," "I'm not good enough," or "Success isn't for people like me," your brain starts to accept those statements as facts. They become internalized limits.

But here's the good news: the opposite is also true.

When you consciously choose to speak powerful, empowering truths, even before you fully believe them, you begin to shift your mindset. You start to walk, talk, and lead like the person you want to become.

Affirmations like:

- "I'm capable of figuring things out."
- "I lead with wisdom and confidence."

- "I attract the right people and the right opportunities."
- "Every setback is a setup for a comeback."

These aren't just motivational slogans, they're seeds. And the more you plant them, water them, and nurture them, the deeper their roots grow. Over time, they start to shape your perspective, influence your choices, and align your behavior with your highest potential.

I've seen this firsthand. When I started repeating affirmations out loud, especially during challenging seasons, I noticed something shift. Not overnight. Not magically. But steadily. I carried myself differently. I took bigger risks with more calm. I approached problems with more creativity. Because I was no longer just reacting to life, I was programming myself to rise to it.

And here's the thing: affirmations aren't about lying to yourself. They're about reminding yourself of what's already possible inside you. They bridge the gap between who you are now and who you're becoming.

Say them when you wake up. Say them before tough meetings. Say them when doubt creeps in. Your words are building the next version of you. Speak wisely, and speak often.

Pairing Belief with Behavior

Affirmations are powerful, but only if they lead to action. You can't just declare, "I'm a successful entrepreneur," and then scroll your day away on social media. You can't say, "I'm confident," and then avoid the phone call that scares you. That's not transformation, that's fantasy.

True growth comes when belief fuels behavior. When the words you speak become a blueprint for how you show up. Affirmations are the foundation, but action is the frame you build on top of it.

Think of it like this: your words are the internal cue, your behavior is the external proof. If the two don't match, your subconscious won't buy in. You'll start to feel dissonance instead of confidence.

Want to be seen as a confident communicator? Start practicing your pitch. Record yourself. Review. Improve.

Want to lead your team with strength and clarity? Stop winging it. Build a plan. Stick to your calendar. Follow through on commitments.

Want to become the kind of person who handles pressure well? Don't just speak peace, choose it in the middle of the storm. Slow your breath. Control your tone. Ground yourself in the moment.

You don't have to be perfect, but you do have to be aligned.

This is where momentum is built, not in the hype of the affirmation, but in the discipline of the follow-through. When your words and actions match, confidence soars. Clarity grows. And people around you start to trust not just what you say, but who you are.

So keep speaking the truth. But more importantly, start walking it out.

Case Study: Jim Carrey and the Power of Visualization

Before Jim Carrey became one of the most recognized comedic actors in the world, he was just another struggling performer in Los Angeles, broke, rejected, and full of uncertainty. But what separated him from so many others chasing the same dream wasn't just his talent. It was his mindset.

In 1990, long before he landed a starring role, Carrey wrote himself a check for $10 million for "acting services rendered." He dated it five years into the future and carried it in his wallet everywhere he went. He wasn't cashing that check, not yet, but he was investing in belief. Every day, he'd drive to Mulholland Drive, park his car, and visualize his success. He'd picture himself being in blockbuster films, being paid what he was worth, and being celebrated for the work he had yet to do.

This wasn't delusion. It was direction. He was training his mind to expect greatness, even before the world saw it in him.

Fast forward five years, almost to the day, Carrey landed the role in Dumb and Dumber, and his paycheck? $10 million.

Now, here's the key: Carrey didn't just speak affirmations into the universe and wait around for a miracle. He worked. He auditioned. He wrote. He hustled. The visualization was the spark, but the grind was the fuel. His belief created clarity. That clarity fueled action. And that action created momentum.

The lesson here isn't that visualization is some kind of shortcut. It's that it creates alignment. It helps you define your target so your effort can hit the mark. When your thoughts, words, and actions all move in the same direction, the compound effect kicks in, and suddenly, the impossible starts to look inevitable.

This mindset isn't just for actors. It's for entrepreneurs, leaders, dreamers, anyone who's building something bigger than what currently exists. Whether your goal is to scale a business, launch a new product, or reinvent your career, visualization is the practice of showing up mentally before you arrive physically.

And if Jim Carrey can go from a broke comedian with a check in his wallet to a global icon with a $10 million payday, maybe, just maybe, there's more power in your thoughts than you think.

Final Thought: Speak Life, Daily

Words create worlds.

Not just in a poetic sense, but in a practical, measurable, transformational way. The words you speak, whether whispered under your breath, repeated silently in your thoughts, or declared boldly in front of a team, shape your perception. And your perception shapes your actions.

This isn't motivational fluff. It's neuroscience. It's behavioral psychology. It's a spiritual truth. Every thought you repeat becomes a belief. Every belief influences a decision. And every decision compounds into a result.

That's why what you say to yourself matters.

Say, "I'm built for this." Not because you feel invincible, but because you're choosing to anchor to resilience.
Say, "I figure things out." Not because the answers are obvious, but because you've decided to become a problem-solver.
Say, "There's always a solution." Not because everything is easy, but because you refuse to let obstacles define your future.

Speak these words before they're true. Speak them when your hands are shaking. Speak them when your confidence is low. Speak them when everything inside you wants to shrink back. Speak them until you believe them. Speak them until your actions match them. Speak them until your world shifts to accommodate them.

You don't have to wait until you feel strong to speak strength.

You speak it first. That's how you become it.

Because your words aren't just commentary. They're construction. Every sentence is a brick. Every affirmation is a beam. Every phrase is a foundation. You're either building a future, or reinforcing a limitation.

So speak life.

Daily.
On purpose.
In the mirror.
In the truck.
In the boardroom.
Before the call.
After the loss.
Right in the middle of the mess.

Your mindset listens.
Your team listens.
Your business listens.

And more than anything, your future listens.

Because when your language aligns with your purpose, your actions start to move with power. And when your actions move with power, results follow. Doors open. People respond. Clarity comes. Energy returns.

So say it like it matters, because it does.

Speak life, and watch what rises in response.

Chapter 6: Setting and Achieving Goals

S uccess in business rarely happens by accident. It's not luck. It's not magic. It's the result of intentional action, driven by clear goals and consistent execution. It's strategy, and strategy begins with clarity.

You don't end up with a thriving company, a strong team, or financial freedom by simply hoping it will happen. Those results come from knowing what you want, defining it clearly, and building toward it, one decision, one habit, one step at a time.

If your mindset is the engine that drives your performance, then your goals are the GPS. They tell you where you're going, how to get there, and how to course-correct when you drift off track. Without goals, you don't steer your business, you react to it. You don't build, you drift. And in business, drift is deadly.

Goals give you focus when distractions come. They give you direction when things feel chaotic. They give you purpose when motivation is low. They remind you why you started, and more importantly, where you're going.

Too many entrepreneurs live in "maintenance mode," just putting out fires and hoping things will improve. But hope is not a strategy. And maintenance isn't momentum. If you're not setting clear goals and chasing them down with intention, you're not leading, you're coasting.

This chapter is about making sure that doesn't happen. It's about giving you a framework to turn your vision into results. Because the future you want won't arrive by accident, it will arrive because you built it, goal by goal.

Why Most People Fail at Goal-Setting

It's not that people don't want to succeed. Most entrepreneurs are driven. They're hungry. They have a vision of something better. But the gap between dreaming and doing is often filled with confusion and chaos.

Here's why most people don't hit their goals:

- **The goal isn't clear.** Vague goals produce vague results. "Make more money" or "grow the business" sounds good, but what does that actually mean? How much? By when? How will you know you've succeeded?

- **The goal isn't theirs.** Too often, we set goals based on what looks good on social media, what other people expect, or what the industry says we should want. But if a goal doesn't resonate with your values or your vision, you won't stay committed when it gets hard.

- **The goal isn't written down.** Studies have shown that you're significantly more likely to achieve a goal simply by writing it down. Why? Because it moves the idea from your imagination into something tangible. It becomes a declaration.

- **The goal isn't broken into action steps.** A goal without a plan is just a wish. If you don't know what to do on Monday morning to move toward that goal, it won't happen. You need a roadmap, not just a destination.

- **The goal gets buried by busywork.** Every day, you're hit with emails, calls, meetings, and problems. If your goals aren't front and center, they'll get pushed to the background. Urgency will always crowd out importance, unless you fight to keep your goals in the spotlight.

It's not willpower that most people are missing, it's a system. They don't need more motivation, they need more clarity. More structure. More follow-through.

That's where a simple, effective goal-setting framework makes all the difference. When you know exactly what you're aiming for, why it matters, and what to do next, the excuses shrink and the progress starts stacking up.

SMART Goals: The Blueprint

If you want your goals to work for you, they need structure. That's where the SMART framework comes in. It takes your vague ambition and gives it bones, something you can build on. SMART goals aren't just motivational, they're actionable. They hold you accountable and give you a clear playbook for success.

Here's how it breaks down:

- **Specific** – What exactly do you want to achieve? Avoid general statements like "grow the business" or "be more successful." Instead, zero in on the outcome. Do you want to increase revenue? Launch a new product? Expand into a new market? Clarity fuels action.

- **Measurable** – How will you track your progress? What are the metrics? Revenue, leads, conversions, hours worked, tasks completed, whatever it is, make sure you can measure it. If you can't measure it, you can't manage it.

- **Achievable** – Is this realistic with the time, resources, and team you have? It should stretch you, but not break you. Overreaching can be as paralyzing as under-aiming. Set goals that are challenging but doable with focused effort.

- **Relevant** – Does this goal align with your bigger vision? A goal that doesn't serve your mission will eventually become a distraction. Make sure it supports your broader business objectives and long-term direction.

- **Time-Bound** – What's the deadline? Without a time frame, a goal becomes a "someday" project. Put a date on it. Set a finish line. Deadlines create urgency and momentum.

Let's take a common example:

- **Bad goal:** "Get more clients."
- **SMART goal:** "Sign five new clients in the next 60 days by increasing

weekly outreach by 25% and launching a referral incentive program."

See the difference? One is a wish. The other is a strategy.

SMART goals force you to think like a business owner, not just a dreamer. They move you from intention to execution. And in entrepreneurship, execution is everything.

Reverse Engineering: The CEO's Mindset

Setting a goal is just the beginning. Achieving it requires a different level of thinking, strategic thinking. That's where reverse engineering comes in. It's the process of starting with your desired outcome and working backward to identify every step required to make it real.

Let's say your goal is to generate $500,000 in revenue over the next 12 months. On the surface, that might feel like a massive mountain. But when you break it down, it becomes much more manageable:

- **Annually:** $500,000

- **Quarterly:** $125,000

- **Monthly:** Just over $41,000

- **Weekly:** Around $10,250

Now ask yourself:

- **What product or service will generate that revenue?** Do you need to sell 50 units of a $10,000 product? Or 500 units of a $1,000 service?

- **How many customers or clients do you need to reach that volume?** What's your average transaction size or customer lifetime value?

- **What kind of outreach or marketing activity is needed to acquire that number of customers?** How many calls, emails, meetings, proposals?

- **What systems or team members are necessary to support that growth?** Where are the gaps in your current structure?

This is how CEOs think. They don't just hope for big results, they map the path. They don't look at the goal and feel overwhelmed. They look at the goal and immediately start deconstructing it into its component parts.

When you break the big goal into bite-sized, time-bound steps, you give yourself a plan. You take control of your growth. And more importantly, you move out of a reactive state and into a proactive one.

Reverse engineering is the bridge between vision and execution. It's what turns good ideas into great outcomes.

Micro Goals: The Power of Small Wins

Big goals can be paralyzing. When you stare at the mountain, it's easy to get overwhelmed and freeze. That's where micro goals come in, they shrink the mountain into manageable steps. They give you something to grab onto today, not "someday."

Micro goals are the daily, bite-sized actions that move you forward without triggering resistance or burnout. They're not about doing less, they're about building momentum in a sustainable way.

Want to write a book? Don't focus on the 60,000 words. Set a micro goal: **Write 300 words a day.** That's one page. Do that consistently and the book will write itself.

Want to get in shape? Don't obsess over the perfect workout plan. Start with a micro goal: **Walk 30 minutes every morning.** Movement leads to motivation.

Want to grow your business? Don't obsess over revenue targets. Focus on a micro goal: **Make 3 outreach calls before 10 a.m. every weekday.** Small moves, big impact.

Micro goals do three powerful things:

1. **Create Momentum** – Once you're in motion, it's easier to stay in motion. Micro goals make it easy to start.

2. **Build Confidence** – Every win, even a small one, signals progress. And progress breeds belief.

3. **Reduce Resistance** – Big goals invite hesitation. Small goals lower the psychological barrier to action.

Micro goals turn intention into motion. They remove the excuse of "I don't have time" or "I don't know where to start." You don't need to overhaul your life in a day. You just need to stack enough small wins until the breakthrough becomes inevitable.

Because the truth is, nobody moves a mountain in one push. They move it one shovel at a time.

Accountability and Tracking

Setting goals is the first step. But if you don't track them and stay accountable to them, they quickly become wishes instead of commitments.

Write your goals down. Not just once in a notebook you'll never open again, write them somewhere you'll see them daily. Your phone wallpaper, a whiteboard in your office, a sticky note on your bathroom mirror. Visibility fuels focus. When your goals are in front of you, they stay top of mind.

Review them often. A goal you don't revisit is a goal you'll eventually forget. Take time weekly to check in. Are you on track? What needs to adjust? This isn't about shame, it's about clarity.

Share your goals with someone who will hold you to them. That could be a coach, a mentor, a business partner, a close friend, or a spouse. Choose someone who knows how to call you up, not just comfort you. Someone who isn't afraid to challenge you when you're coasting, and who genuinely wants to see you win.

Tracking doesn't need to be complicated. Use what works for you, a spreadsheet, a notes app, a journal, a project management tool. What matters most is consistency. Build a rhythm around it. Make it a habit.

And above all, **be honest**. You can't grow from what you won't admit. Tracking is your mirror. It reveals the truth about where your energy is going, what's working, and what's not.

Because what gets measured gets managed. And what gets managed gets mastered.

When Goals Need to Change

One of the most overlooked skills in entrepreneurship is knowing when to pivot, not because you're quitting, but because you're growing.

Sometimes, a goal that once inspired you no longer fits the direction your life or business is heading. Maybe your priorities changed. Maybe new information came to light. Maybe the market shifted. That's not failure, that's wisdom.

But here's the catch: **don't confuse friction with a dead end.** There's a difference between a goal that's no longer aligned and a goal that's simply uncomfortable. The former deserves a re-evaluation. The latter often just requires grit.

Before walking away from a goal, ask yourself:

- **Is this still tied to my core values?**
- **Is this goal still in alignment with my long-term vision?**
- **Am I pivoting from wisdom or running from difficulty?**

If the goal no longer fits who you're becoming or where you're headed, give yourself permission to adjust. That's strategic. But if you're just tired or discouraged, double down on your discipline before you abandon the direction.

Change the timeline. Change the tactics. But protect the vision.

Because great entrepreneurs don't blindly stick to a plan just to prove a point, they evolve. They adapt. And when it's time to release a goal, they do it without guilt, knowing they're making room for something better.

Case Study: John Doerr and Google's OKRs

In the late 1990s, Google was a young, scrappy startup with big dreams. They had brilliant engineers, a revolutionary search algorithm, and a vision to "organize the world's information." But like many fast-growing companies, they lacked structure. That's where John Doerr came in.

Doerr, a legendary venture capitalist at Kleiner Perkins, had learned the power of strategic goal-setting during his time at Intel. He introduced Google's founders, Larry Page and Sergey Brin, to a system called OKRs, Objectives and Key Results.

Unlike traditional goal-setting methods, OKRs were designed to drive focus, alignment, and measurable progress. Every team at Google was encouraged to set ambitious, qualitative objectives, clear, motivating statements of what they wanted to achieve. Then they paired each objective with 3–5 key results, specific, measurable outcomes that defined what success looked like.

For example:

- **Objective:** Make Google the fastest search engine in the world.
  - **Key Result 1:** Reduce average search response time by 50%.
  - **Key Result 2:** Launch data center upgrades across North America.
  - **Key Result 3:** Improve server processing speed by 25%.

The brilliance of OKRs wasn't just in setting goals, it was in creating transparency. Everyone's OKRs were visible across the company. That meant a junior engineer could see what the CEO was focused on, and align their work accordingly. It also meant progress was tracked, celebrated, and evaluated without micromanagement or guesswork.

Under this system, Google didn't just grow, they scaled with intention. They stayed agile, adapted quickly, and remained aligned across thousands of employees, departments, and global offices.

John Doerr would later say, "Ideas are easy. Execution is everything." And OKRs gave Google the structure to execute their world-changing ideas.

The takeaway? When your goals are clear, your team is focused, and your results are measured, growth becomes scalable, and vision becomes reality.

Final Thought: Goals Aren't Just About Achievement, They're About Identity

The true power of a goal isn't in the result, it's in the transformation that happens along the way. It's not about the number on the spreadsheet or the title on your business card. It's about who you become in the process of pursuing something meaningful.

When you set a goal, you're not just setting a target. You're making a declaration: "This is the kind of person I want to be." Focused. Disciplined. Strategic. Resilient. The goal is the outer expression, but the real change happens inside you.

The late Jim Rohn once said, "Set the kind of goals that will make something of you to achieve them." That's it. The goal is the vehicle, character is the destination.

Want to hit a new revenue milestone? You'll have to become someone who thinks bigger, manages better, and leads stronger. Want to build a team? You'll have to become someone who communicates clearly, coaches consistently, and sets high standards. Want to create more freedom in your life? You'll have to become someone who's better at systems, boundaries, and long-term planning.

That's why vague goals fail. They don't demand a new version of you. But when you set bold, clear goals, you trigger growth by necessity.

So don't just ask yourself, "What do I want to accomplish?" Ask, "Who must I become to accomplish it?"

Then get to work. Start showing up like that person. Make decisions from that identity. Speak like them. Act like them. Think like them. Because over time, you won't just reach the goal, you'll become someone who can reach bigger ones.

And that, ultimately, is the real win.

Chapter 7: Building Confidence

If mindset is the engine, then confidence is the ignition switch. You can have the best strategies, the smartest plans, and the most innovative ideas, but without confidence, none of it gets off the ground. Confidence is what gets you to step up, speak out, and swing when the opportunity comes your way.

But let's get something straight: confidence isn't arrogance. It's not puffing your chest out or pretending to have all the answers. Real confidence is quiet. It's grounded. It's the calm assurance that you'll figure it out, even if you don't know how yet. It's the belief that your potential is greater than your current performance, and that your future is bigger than your fear.

Too many people wait for confidence to show up before they move. They think, "Once I feel more secure, more prepared, more worthy, then I'll go for it." But that's not how it works. Confidence doesn't come before the leap. It comes after. You build it through action, through repetition, through showing up even when you're scared.

And here's the part most people miss: confidence isn't something you're born with. It's not reserved for the lucky or the loud. It's a skill. Like public speaking. Like sales. Like leadership. It's something you train, something you earn, something you grow.

Confidence is built, not bestowed. And the sooner you stop waiting for it and start working on it, the faster everything else will start to move.

Confidence Comes from Doing, Not Wishing

Confidence doesn't show up just because you want it to. It doesn't come from watching another TED Talk, listening to a podcast, or scrolling through a highlight reel on social media. Inspiration might spark the fire, but it's action that keeps it burning.

Confidence is built in the doing. In the messy, uncertain, imperfect steps you take while still feeling unsure. It's not the absence of fear, it's the decision to act anyway. Every time you push through the discomfort, every time you try something new, every time you get back up after falling flat, you collect evidence. And that evidence slowly rewires your brain.

You go from "I don't know if I can" to "Maybe I can." From "I've never done this before" to "I've done hard things before, I can figure this out too." That's how belief is built, not in theory, but in practice.

I've had to learn this the hard way. There were times I wanted confidence to just show up. I wanted to feel ready, feel bold, feel unshakable. But what I found is that confidence never pre-approved my moves. It showed up after I made them. After I picked up the phone. After I had the uncomfortable conversation. After I put myself out there.

And that's the truth most people don't want to hear: confidence is earned. One action at a time. One brave step at a time. You want more confidence? Do more things that scare you. Get in the game. Collect the evidence. And watch who you become.

A Lesson in Listening

If I've struggled with anything over the years, it hasn't been a lack of confidence, it's been too much of it. I've always believed I could figure things out. That I could build a business from scratch. That I could lead a team, solve a problem, close a deal. And most of the time, that belief gave me an edge. It pushed me to act when others hesitated. It helped me charge into situations that required guts and grit.

But like most strengths, when left unchecked, that confidence started drifting into something else: arrogance. And it took a jarring moment for me to see it.

I was with a group of friends, venting about a frustrating conversation I'd had earlier that day. I was animated, telling the story like I was in a courtroom, making my case, proving my point. I thought they'd back me up. Instead, one of them turned to another and said, with a smirk, "Didn't they realize who they were talking to? You're Michael Allen!" Everyone laughed.

Except me.

They thought it was funny. I heard the truth in it. That offhand joke landed like a punch to the gut. These were people I admired. People whose respect I valued. And in that moment, I realized they didn't just see me as confident, they saw me as full of myself. As someone more interested in being right than being real. As someone who had more mouth than humility.

That moment stayed with me.

It was the wake-up call I didn't know I needed. Confidence without humility is just noise. It demands attention instead of earning respect. Real confidence doesn't announce itself. It doesn't need to dominate the conversation or defend every move. It lets the work speak. It lets the impact speak.

From that day forward, I made a shift. I started listening more than I talked. I paid closer attention to how I carried myself, not just in business, but in every room I walked into. I traded the urge to prove for the desire to understand. And I let my results, not my mouth, do the talking.

That decision didn't shrink my confidence. It deepened it. Because when you root your confidence in humility, it doesn't get shaken by criticism. It grows from it.

Confidence and Evidence

Confidence isn't wishful thinking, it's built on evidence. It's not about convincing yourself you're capable; it's about showing yourself. It's about creating a track record of follow-through, discipline, and resilience that you can look back on and say, "I've done hard things before, I can do this too."

Think about it like building a case in court. Every time you do what you said you'd do, you're submitting evidence to the jury in your mind. Every time you honor a commitment, however small, you're stacking proof in your favor.

You said you'd wake up early, did you hit snooze or hit the ground running? You committed to making 10 sales calls, did you power through, or put it off? You promised to finish the proposal by Friday, was it done, or still sitting untouched?

Each of these moments matters. Not because anyone else sees them, but because you do. You are always watching yourself. And your brain takes notes.

When you consistently follow through, you begin to trust yourself at a deep level. That trust is what fuels real confidence. Not bravado. Not hype. Just steady, quiet evidence that you are who you say you are.

And here's the good news: it works both ways. Even if you've broken promises in the past, you can start rebuilding that trust today. One small win at a time. One action followed by another. You don't need to be perfect. You just need to be consistent.

Because confidence isn't something you find. It's something you prove. One kept promise at a time.

Comparison is the Confidence Killer

If there's one habit guaranteed to erode your confidence, it's comparison. And in today's world, it's easier, and more dangerous, than ever. With just a few swipes, you can see someone else's success, lifestyle, revenue wins, perfect branding, or team growth. But what you're really seeing is the highlight reel, not the full story.

You don't see the sleepless nights, the failed launches, the tears behind the scenes, or the self-doubt that kept them up at 3 a.m. You see the polished version, edited for impact and filtered through success. And when you measure your behind-the-scenes against someone else's best moments, you'll always feel like you're losing.

This is especially toxic in entrepreneurship, where progress isn't always linear. One month you're up. The next, you're scrambling. That's normal. That's part of the game. But if you're always scanning sideways, you'll miss what's happening in front of you. You'll question your path. You'll rush decisions.

You'll chase validation instead of vision.

Confidence doesn't grow from comparison, it grows from clarity. From knowing who you are, what you're building, and why it matters. It comes from defining success on your own terms, not someone else's timeline.

So stop asking, "Am I where they are?" Start asking, "Am I further than I was?" That's the real test. That's the real win.

Run your race. Own your pace. And remember: confidence isn't about being ahead of others, it's about becoming better than who you were yesterday.

Tools to Build Real Confidence

Confidence isn't a personality trait, it's a practice. It's not reserved for the loudest voice in the room or the most outgoing person at the table. It's available to anyone willing to build it on purpose. Here are some tools that have helped me, and can help you too:

1. Small Wins, Big Momentum

Don't underestimate the power of small, consistent victories. When you set and achieve tiny, daily goals, like making the call, finishing the email, showing up on time, you build trust with yourself. Every win, no matter how small, becomes a deposit in your confidence bank. Over time, that account grows. You start to believe in your ability to follow through, and that belief fuels even bigger wins.

2. Rewire Negative Self-Talk

We all have that inner critic, the voice that whispers, "You're not good enough," or "You're going to blow this." The goal isn't to silence it completely, it's to override it. When that voice shows up, counter it with truth. Say, "I've faced worse," or "I'm learning," or "I know what I bring to the table." With practice, your new voice becomes louder than the old one.

3. Dress and Speak the Part

Confidence starts before you speak. It's in how you walk, how you carry yourself, how you enter the room. Your body sends signals to your brain. When you stand tall, make eye contact, and speak with intention, your brain starts to believe you belong. It's not about faking it, it's about aligning your posture with your purpose.

4. Audit Your Circle

Confidence grows in the right environment. If you're constantly surrounded by people who belittle your dreams or second-guess your decisions, you'll start to absorb that doubt. But if you're around builders, people who encourage, challenge, and support, you'll rise to meet their energy. Take inventory. Your circle should be a greenhouse, not a graveyard.

5. Prepare Like a Pro

Preparation breeds confidence. When you've done the work, rehearsed the pitch, studied the numbers, built the plan, you walk in different. You're not guessing. You're grounded. The people who seem "naturally" confident usually aren't, they're just better prepared. So put in the reps. Do your homework. Confidence follows effort. These tools aren't complicated, but they are powerful. And when you use them daily, confidence becomes more than a feeling, it becomes your foundation.

Case Study:
Howard Schultz and Starbucks

Before Starbucks became a household name, it was just a small chain of coffee shops in Seattle selling beans and equipment, not drinks. Howard Schultz was a marketing executive at the time, working for Starbucks and inspired by a trip he took to Italy. There, he discovered something different: the café culture. People weren't just grabbing coffee, they were gathering, connecting, unwinding. Schultz saw more than a beverage. He saw an experience. And he wanted to bring it home.

But when he pitched his idea, transforming Starbucks into a coffeehouse experience built around community and premium espresso drinks, the founders said no. They didn't see the vision. They didn't want to change the model. So Schultz left the company and set out to build his own version of the idea. But he needed funding. And that's where the real test began.

Investor after investor turned him down. Over 200 rejections. Some said coffee was too niche. Others said Americans wouldn't pay for something they could get for free at home. Some just didn't believe Schultz had the chops to build something that big. The doubts were constant. The rejections personal.

But Schultz didn't crumble. He refined his pitch. He studied the market. He built financial models. He anticipated objections. He kept showing up.

Eventually, he raised enough money to open Il Giornale, his own coffee shop based on the Italian espresso bar. It was a hit. So when Starbucks came up for sale, Schultz bought it, and began transforming it into the global brand we know today.

Here's the key: Schultz didn't succeed because he had all the answers from the start. He succeeded because he had unwavering belief paired with consistent, courageous action. He was rejected, underestimated, and told he was wrong more times than most people could stomach. But he believed in the mission. He believed in himself. And he believed that the world would eventually catch up.

That's real confidence. Not noise. Not ego. Just the steady, grounded conviction that what you're building matters, even when no one else sees it yet.

And it's a lesson for every entrepreneur: You don't need everyone to believe. You just need to believe long enough to prove it.

Final Thought: Become the Proof

You don't need someone else to tell you you're enough. You don't need a title, a trophy, or a round of applause to validate your worth. What you need is evidence, evidence that you can do hard things, face big fears, and rise when it would be easier to retreat.

You need to become the proof.

Do the work, not for show, but for strength. Keep your word, not just to others, but to yourself. Take the shot, even when the target feels out of reach. Because every time you follow through on a promise, every time you show up when it's easier to stay hidden, every time you stretch beyond what's comfortable, you're casting a vote for the kind of person you're becoming.

Confidence isn't something you wait to feel. It's something you build, one decision at a time.

You become powerful not because everything goes right, but because you choose to keep going when things go wrong. You become grounded not because you never waver, but because you return to your values when you do.

So stop looking for proof outside of yourself. Stop waiting for someone else to anoint you as ready. Start becoming the kind of leader, entrepreneur, and person you admire, through your choices, through your effort, through your consistency.

You don't need permission. You need momentum.

And it starts the moment you stop trying to be impressive, and start aiming to be undeniable.

Chapter 8: Overcoming Negative Money Thoughts

Money isn't just about dollars and cents, it's about mindset. For entrepreneurs, money carries emotional weight. It's rarely neutral. It gets tangled up in memories, expectations, and beliefs handed down by parents, teachers, culture, and experience. It can trigger fear, guilt, insecurity, shame, or even self-sabotage. And if you don't deal with your money mindset, it will quietly run the show.

You can be brilliant. You can have the best product on the market. You can build a killer strategy. But if there's a part of you that doesn't believe you're worthy of earning, growing, or keeping money, you'll sabotage your own success. You'll undercharge. You'll overdeliver. You'll downplay your value. And the worst part? You won't even realize you're doing it.

This isn't just about profit margins or pricing models. It's about identity. It's about the stories you tell yourself about what you're allowed to have, who you're allowed to become, and what success should look like.

That's why healing your relationship with money isn't a luxury, it's a necessity. It's not something you get to later, once you're successful. It's the work that creates success in the first place.

Because when you fix your mindset around money, everything else gets easier. You stop operating from fear. You stop avoiding hard financial conversations. You start making decisions with clarity, confidence, and purpose.

You stop chasing money, and start commanding it.

My Relationship with Money

I didn't grow up wealthy. In fact, like many people, I grew up watching my mother stretch every dollar just to keep the lights on. She worked multiple jobs, not for luxury, but for survival. That was my first exposure to money: not as a tool, but as a tension. Something to be earned, chased, stretched, and feared.

But everything began to shift when I was around ten years old. That's when Danny came into our lives. He married my mom, brought stability, and introduced a new rhythm to our home, one that included not just hard work, but smart work. Danny was in the scrap metal business, and through him, I saw money from a different lens. It wasn't just something you earned hourly, it was something you could build, trade, invest, and multiply.

We weren't rich. We didn't live extravagantly. But we had enough. And most importantly, we had options. That's what money really is, options. The ability to make decisions based on values, not just survival.

As I got older, life did what it does. It humbled me. After serving in the Army, I came home and struggled to find stable work. I had a truck repossessed. I had bills I couldn't pay and days where I didn't know what was coming next. But here's what never changed: I never saw myself as helpless. I didn't shrink into scarcity. I always believed there was a way forward, I just had to find it.

That belief was rooted in one simple truth I've carried with me ever since: money isn't scarce. It's everywhere. It moves in and out of hands, businesses, and banks at breathtaking speed. The problem isn't that there isn't enough, the problem is most people don't know how to position themselves to receive it.

I'll give you a picture that reshaped my entire understanding of wealth.

Imagine graduating high school and landing a job that pays $1 million a year. No college. No debt. You live like a monk. Save every penny. Invest smartly. After 50 years, you retire with a net worth of $100 million. Sounds like a fantasy, right?

Now, picture yourself at an art auction where a single painting, just canvas and paint, is sold for $110 million.

Let that sink in.

A person could live the most disciplined financial life imaginable and still not afford one luxury item that someone else bought casually.

That's when I stopped thinking of wealth as a finish line and started seeing it as an ocean. It's out there, massive, moving, abundant. The key isn't to hoard it or hope for it. The key is to understand it. To learn how to step into the current and build something that attracts and directs it.

From that point on, I stopped asking, "How do I get more money?" and started asking, "How do I manage it better? How do I align my mindset, habits, and strategy with the flow of abundance?"

That shift, from scarcity to strategy, from earning to stewarding, was the beginning of everything changing for me.

Money Is a Mirror

Money doesn't change you. It reveals you.

That might sound cliché, but in business and in life, I've found it to be undeniably true. Money has a way of amplifying whatever is already inside you. It doesn't create character, it exposes it. It doesn't bring wisdom, it tests it.

If you're generous when you have little, you'll be even more generous when you have a lot. If you're disciplined with a small budget, you'll likely make smart choices with a larger one. If you're intentional, strategic, and grateful with $10,000, you'll be all those things with $100,000 or more.

But the reverse is also true.

If you're anxious about money when you don't have much, that anxiety won't disappear with more zeros in your account. If you're careless, impulsive, or driven by ego when you're just starting out, money will only make those habits more dangerous. It shines a light on your blind spots and multiplies your habits, good or bad.

That's why I always tell people: your money mindset is more important than your math skills. Yes, you need to understand numbers. Yes, profit and loss matter. But if your internal beliefs about money are broken, if you believe you're not worthy, that success is suspect, that ambition is selfish, then no amount of financial knowledge will keep you from sabotaging yourself.

You'll undercharge. Overwork. Overgive. Undervalue.

Because money is more than a metric, it's a mirror. It reflects your beliefs, your priorities, your fears, and your identity.

That's why so many people earn well and still feel broke. Because it's not about income, it's about alignment. You have to align your mindset with the level of wealth you want to create and sustain.

So here's the real question: What is your money revealing about you?
Are you afraid to charge what you're worth?
Do you feel guilt when you succeed?
Are you stuck in a cycle of feast and famine because deep down, you believe you don't deserve stability?

None of these questions are meant to shame you. They're meant to free you. Because once you become aware of what money is mirroring back to you, you can change the reflection.

You can start telling a new story. One where money isn't the villain or the goal, it's the fuel. The resource. The magnifier of your purpose.

Money is a tool. A lever. A servant, not a master. It's neutral. You decide what it amplifies. You decide what it builds. You decide how it shows up in your life and in your legacy.

And that starts by getting your mindset right.

The Most Dangerous Thought: "I'm Not Worth That"

This is the mindset that derails more entrepreneurs than inflation, competition, or even bad business models. Not lack of talent. Not lack of opportunity. But the quiet, corrosive belief: "I'm not worth that much."

It shows up in subtle ways: hesitation when quoting a price. Nervousness when discussing rates. Discounts that no one asked for. An invoice that goes unsent because you don't want to seem greedy. You say it's strategy, but deep down, it's fear.

And I've seen it over and over again.

I've worked with leaders who deliver massive value. They change lives, solve big problems, and move the needle for their clients. But when it comes time to talk money, they shrink. They tiptoe around their prices. They justify their worth with insecurity disguised as humility.

That's not humility. That's a lie. A lie too many entrepreneurs were taught to believe.

They were told that "good people" don't care about money. That wanting more makes you selfish. That charging high rates is arrogant. That asking for what you're worth is somehow wrong.

Let me tell you something plainly: it's not.

True humility isn't about hiding your worth. It's about honoring it. It's about showing up in the fullness of your gift, delivering excellence, and expecting to be compensated accordingly, not because you're better than anyone else, but because value deserves value in return.

When you undercharge out of fear, you're not serving your clients, you're shortchanging them. You're modeling scarcity. You're reinforcing shame. You're teaching them that transformation should come cheap. And you're setting a ceiling, not just for yourself, but for the people who are watching how you lead.

Pricing isn't just a business decision. It's a mindset declaration.

It says, "I believe in the work I do."
"I believe in the results I help create."
"I believe that excellence deserves to be rewarded."

And if you don't believe that yet, start practicing until you do. Because when you do, everything changes.

You attract clients who take the work seriously. You build a business that sustains you. You stop chasing scraps and start building something scalable. You don't just build revenue, you build respect.

So here's the truth: You're not charging for your time. You're charging for your transformation. For the years it took to gain your skill. For the problems you know how to solve. For the breakthrough your clients couldn't get without you.

Stop apologizing for that.

You're not just worth it. You're responsible for acting like it.

My Mindset Reset

I've never really struggled with the belief that I bring value. That part came naturally to me. I've always had a sense of what I could contribute, what I was capable of, and what my time and effort were worth. If anything, my challenge wasn't in believing I was worth it, it was in learning how to channel that belief into sustainable action. The lesson I had to learn wasn't confidence, it was stewardship.

Early in my journey, I treated money like momentum: get it fast, spend it fast, reinvest it fast, grow fast. That kind of pace works in short bursts, but it's not sustainable. It doesn't build long-term freedom. It builds burnout. I wasn't building a financial legacy, I was chasing one.

The shift started when I realized that money isn't something to chase. It's something to command. To manage with discipline. To multiply with intention.

I stopped romanticizing big wins and started focusing on smart ones.

I began studying wealth, not the highlight reels of people flaunting cars and vacations, but real, generational wealth. The kind built on assets, not attention. I studied how wealthy families structured their businesses, diversified their income, and prepared for downturns. I stopped asking, "How much did I make this month?" and started asking, "How much stayed? Where did it go? What is it building?"

I started tracking cash flow religiously. I looked at every dollar in and every dollar out. Not from a place of scarcity, but from a place of responsibility. I looked for inefficiencies, for leaks, for habits that didn't match my goals.

I invested time into learning about money management, tax strategy, investment vehicles, and risk mitigation. I started treating every dollar like a seed, not just to spend or save, but to sow. To grow something that could last. Something that could scale. Something that could support my vision without constantly requiring my hustle.

That mindset reset didn't just improve my bottom line, it gave me peace. Peace of mind that I was building something with structure. Confidence that I wasn't just moving money, I was multiplying it. And most of all, clarity that I wasn't just hustling for a paycheck, I was building a platform for legacy.

That's what stewardship is about. Not managing from fear, but leading your finances with vision. With maturity. With purpose.

Because at the end of the day, wealth isn't just about what you earn. It's about what you build. And who you become in the process.

Case Study: Ramit Sethi and the Psychology of Wealth

Ramit Sethi, the bestselling author of I Will Teach You To Be Rich, didn't build his reputation by teaching people how to pinch pennies, he built it by helping them rewire their thinking around money. Where most financial advice starts with restriction, Sethi starts with permission. His message is clear: wealth isn't about deprivation, it's about design.

Sethi discovered early on that the real problem wasn't just that people didn't know how to manage their money, it was that they were stuck in psychological loops of guilt, fear, and shame. They weren't just making bad financial decisions, they were making emotionally driven ones.

He noticed that people would obsess over $3 lattes but avoid the uncomfortable conversation about why they weren't earning more, investing, or pursuing higher-value opportunities. He challenged this thinking head-on.

Instead of telling people to cut back on everything, Sethi flipped the script. He introduced the idea of a "rich life," customized to each person's values. For some, that meant travel. For others, it meant convenience, generosity, or luxury experiences. His point? You don't have to feel bad about spending, you just have to spend intentionally.

And more than anything, Sethi's work emphasized the power of automation and systems. He taught that you don't rise to the level of your goals, you fall to the level of your systems. His readers and students learned to set up automated investments, bills, and savings plans so that wealth-building happened in the background, not through sheer willpower.

What makes Sethi's case especially powerful for entrepreneurs is his take on self-worth. He regularly coaches freelancers, coaches, and creatives who undervalue their work. His direct, sometimes blunt advice? Raise your prices. Own your expertise. Stop negotiating with yourself.

He doesn't just focus on earning more, he focuses on earning confidently. On shedding the fear of being "too expensive" and stepping into the truth that your skills, time, and energy are worth charging for. Loudly. Proudly. Without apology.

In a world full of financial fear-mongering, Sethi's voice stands out because it's rooted in empowerment. He reminds us that money doesn't start in the wallet, it starts in the mind. And if you can upgrade your thinking, your income will follow.

That's a lesson every entrepreneur needs: wealth is built by people who believe they deserve to build it, and who take aligned action to make it happen.

Five Ways to Heal Your Money Mindset

Your relationship with money is just that, a relationship. And like any relationship, it can be toxic, strained, or filled with fear unless it's examined, understood, and intentionally rebuilt. Healing your money mindset isn't about learning how to save more or spend less, it's about transforming the way you think, feel, and act around money. Here's how to start:

1. Identify the Script

Every belief you have about money came from somewhere, your parents, your culture, your community, your early experiences. The first step to healing is uncovering those invisible scripts.

Ask yourself:

- What did I hear about money growing up?
- Was wealth seen as good, bad, or dangerous?
- Was hard work glorified but wealth demonized?
- Who taught me what was "enough"?

Write those beliefs down. Get them out of your head and onto paper. Then ask the key question: "Is this true, and is it serving me?"

Because you can't rewrite a story you haven't read.

2. Create a New Narrative

Once you've exposed the old script, it's time to write a new one. You're not stuck with the beliefs you inherited. You get to choose what to believe moving forward.

Craft affirmations that reflect where you're going, not where you've been:

- "Money flows to value, and I create massive value."
- "I am a good steward of wealth and use it to do good."
- "There is no limit to what I can earn or build."

Speak them daily. Write them often. Think of them as internal code, your thoughts are the software, and repetition is the update button. Every time you repeat them, you're rewiring your brain to see money through a healthier, more empowering lens.

3. Track What You Want to Grow

You can't master what you won't measure. If you want more money, start treating it like an asset that deserves your full attention.

Track:

- Every dollar in and out
- Revenue sources
- Expenses
- Profit margins
- Investment growth

Not obsessively, but consistently. Because money, like any resource, responds to stewardship. When you pay attention to it, it starts to work for you, not against you.

And remember: tracking isn't about shame. It's about awareness. You don't track to judge yourself. You track to empower yourself.

4. Talk About It

Money thrives in clarity and dies in secrecy. If you want to grow financially, you have to start having honest conversations.

That means:

- Asking mentors how they manage their money
- Comparing notes with trusted peers
- Seeking out a coach or financial advisor
- Admitting when you don't know something

Entrepreneurs especially tend to isolate financially. We pretend we're doing fine while drowning in stress. Don't do that. Create a circle where money talk isn't taboo, it's normal.

Vulnerability is the price of clarity. But once you open up, you'll be shocked how many others are dealing with the same challenges, and how much faster you grow together.

5. Charge for Value, Not Time

One of the biggest mindset shifts you'll ever make is this: your time has value, but your results are priceless.

Stop pricing yourself like a commodity. Start thinking like a creator of transformation.

Don't ask, "How many hours will this take me?"
Ask, "What's the outcome I deliver, and what's that worth to my client?"

When you shift from billing by the hour to pricing based on impact, two things happen:

1. You make more money.
2. You start owning your worth with confidence.

Remember, clients don't care how long it took, they care what changed. And when you charge accordingly, everyone wins.

Final Thought: You Were Meant to Thrive

You weren't built to live paycheck to paycheck. You weren't designed to feel guilty every time you raise your rates or fearful every time you check your bank account. You weren't created just to survive.

You were built to thrive.

To create. To multiply. To steward what you've been given and turn it into something more, something that lasts, something that impacts not just your life but the lives of others.

There's nothing noble about staying small out of fear or shame. There's nothing virtuous about refusing to step into your full financial potential. Money doesn't make you selfish. Misalignment does. But when your heart is in the right place, wealth becomes a weapon for good.

So stop apologizing for wanting more. More stability. More freedom. More opportunities for your family. More impact in your community. Those desires are not wrong. They're a reflection of your vision.

Money is not the mission, but it is the multiplier.

When you master your money mindset, you'll find that you're not just building wealth. You're building confidence. Clarity. Courage. You're creating margin to give, to lead, to rest, to innovate.

This isn't just about earning. It's about expanding, your capacity, your generosity, your leadership.

You were not made to scrape by. You were made to build. To lead. To leave something better than you found it.

So embrace that truth.
You were meant to thrive. And when you fully believe that, everything changes.

Chapter 9: Networking, Relationships, and Mentorship

Success in entrepreneurship isn't a solo endeavor. While the image of the lone entrepreneur forging ahead is romanticized, the rugged individualist who builds an empire from scratch, the reality is far more communal. Behind every thriving business is a web of relationships: mentors who lend wisdom, peers who offer perspective, partners who challenge your thinking, and teammates who help bring the vision to life.

No matter how driven, talented, or visionary you are, there will be moments when you need encouragement, insight, or access that only others can provide. Relationships aren't just nice to have, they're necessary. They're the lever that lifts you when strategy stalls and the compass that steers you when you feel lost. They turn the impossible into a shared challenge and make the journey less isolating and more empowering.

And here's the truth: the higher you climb, the more vital relationships become. The right connection can cut your learning curve in half, help you avoid costly mistakes, and unlock opportunities you wouldn't find on your own.

This chapter isn't just about networking, it's about how to build meaningful, strategic relationships that help you grow as a person, a leader, and a business owner. It's about learning who to trust, how to give, and when to ask. Because the quality of your business is often a reflection of the quality of your connections.

The Power of Strategic Relationships

Throughout my entrepreneurial journey, I've engaged in all kinds of partnerships. I've started businesses with my dad, teamed up with longtime friends, and collaborated with colleagues I deeply respected. Some of those ventures went the distance. Others unraveled. Each one brought a lesson, not just about business, but about people.

Early on, I believed that if you needed help building something, the natural solution was to bring on a partner. It felt fair. Democratic. Safer. But as time passed, I started to see the cracks in that thinking.

The truth is, not every problem requires a partner. Not every skill gap calls for shared ownership. What I really needed, what most entrepreneurs actually need, wasn't someone to co-own the business. It was someone to contribute to the mission. To show up, add value, and execute with excellence. That can be an employee, a contractor, an advisor, or a collaborator, but it doesn't always need to be a co-founder.

Take Christy, for example. She runs one of my businesses like it's her own. She solves problems before I even hear about them. She leads with care and excellence. She's deeply invested in our success, and she doesn't own a single share. Why? Because she doesn't need equity to feel ownership. She needs clarity, trust, and reward. And when you give talented people those three things, they will move mountains for you.

One of the biggest mistakes I see new entrepreneurs make is giving away equity out of fear. Fear of not being enough. Fear of doing it alone. Fear of failing without backup. But here's the hard truth: fear is a terrible business partner.

Equity is expensive. It's not just a share of your profits, it's a share of your control, your vision, your future. You should never give it away just to feel less scared. Give it when it aligns with your long-term goals, when it brings strategic value, and when the person on the other end is truly worth the partnership.

Strategic relationships are about placing people where they thrive, not just where they feel comfortable. It's about matching skill with need, not just matching energy with enthusiasm. It's about being honest with yourself: do I really need a partner, or do I need a player who can run their lane with excellence?

The more I've learned to build roles instead of defaulting to partnerships, the stronger, leaner, and more focused my businesses have become. Ownership isn't the only path to commitment. And when you learn to deploy relationships strategically, you unlock a whole new level of freedom and performance.

Building a Robust Network

A strong network is one of the most valuable assets an entrepreneur can build. But let's be clear, networking isn't about passing out business cards at random events or flooding inboxes with cold pitches. It's not about collecting names. It's about cultivating relationships that matter. Relationships rooted in trust, respect, and shared value.

In my experience, the most impactful opportunities didn't come from fancy marketing campaigns or pitch decks, they came from people. A recommendation from a peer. A warm intro from a mentor. A challenge from a friend that pushed me to level up. Business moves at the speed of trust, and trust is built through consistent, meaningful connection.

Effective networking involves a few key disciplines:

1. Intentional Engagement
Don't show up just to be seen, show up with purpose. Whether it's an industry conference, a mastermind, a chamber of commerce meeting, or an online forum, know why you're there and what you bring to the table. Have a clear sense of your goals, your value, and the kind of relationships you're looking to build. Show up prepared, present, and curious.

2. Authentic Connections
Forget the pitch. Start with the person. Ask better questions. Listen more than you talk. Find common ground. People can smell desperation or manipulation from a mile away. But when you lead with sincerity and service, you stand out, and people remember you. Your goal isn't just to be liked. It's to be respected and remembered for the right reasons.

3. Reciprocity
The best networks are built on give and take, but the giving always comes

first. Share what you know. Make the introduction. Offer encouragement. Recommend a tool. Celebrate a win. People remember who helped them, who believed in them, who made life a little easier without asking for anything in return. Those are the connections that last.

4. Consistency

Don't wait until you need something to reach out. Stay connected. Send a message just to check in. Share an article they'd appreciate. Comment on their success. Networking is like farming, not hunting. Plant seeds, water them, and be patient. The harvest always comes, often when you least expect it.

5. Diversity of Perspectives

Don't limit your network to people just like you. Seek out people in different industries, at different stages of the journey, with different worldviews. That's where real lear ing happens. That's where creativity is sparked. A well-rounded network stretches you and protects you from blind spots.

Your network is more than a list of names, it's a living, breathing ecosystem of people who can sharpen you, challenge you, support you, and grow with you. And if you treat those relationships with the care they deserve, they'll become one of the most important assets in your business and your life.

The Role of Mentorship

Mentorship is one of the most underrated accelerators in entrepreneurship. A great mentor won't just give you advice, they'll give you perspective. They've walked the path you're trying to walk. They've faced the challenges you'r facing now. And their experience can help you avoid costly mistakes, take smarter risks, and make faster progress.

In my own journey, I've been fortunate to have mentors who poured into me, some formally, most informally. These were people who didn't just share what to do; they showed me how to think. They helped me zoom out when I was too close to the problem. They called me out when I was playing small. They challenged me to grow into the next version of myself.

Finding the right mentor involves more than just asking someone successful to guide you. It requires clarity, initiative, and humility.

Here's what I've learned:

1. Identify Your Needs
Before seeking a mentor, get clear on where you need help. Are you struggling with leadership? Scaling? Finances? Hiring? Don't just look for someone successful, look for someone who has mastered what you're trying to learn. That alignment creates more meaningful mentorship.

2. Build Real Relationships
The best mentorships grow organically. They often start with a conversation, not a contract. Buy someone lunch. Ask thoughtful questions. Show genuine interest in their story. When they see that you're serious, that you take action on their advice, they'll be more likely to invest in you. Mentorship is earned, not assigned.

3. Be Coachable
This is a big one. Nothing will shut down a mentor faster than someone who's defensive, dismissive, or always "knows better." If you want someone to pour into you, show them it's worth their time. Take notes. Follow up. Circle back with updates. Let them see their investment paying off through your growth.

4. Add Value Back
You might not be able to repay a mentor financially, but you can always offer gratitude, effort, and respect. Share resources they'd appreciate. Offer support in their ventures. Promote their work. Even a handwritten thank-you note goes a long way. Remember, mentors are people too, and they want to feel valued, not used.

5. Don't Cling, Climb
A mentor's job isn't to carry you, it's to equip you. Don't become dependent. Use the wisdom they share to elevate your own thinking, then act on it. As you grow, your relationship with your mentor should evolve too, from student to peer, and in time, to mentor yourself.

The best mentors don't just teach, they believe in you. And sometimes, that belief is the very thing that propels you forward when nothing else will. So seek mentorship intentionally, nurture those relationships, and when the time comes, pay it forward. Because success isn't just about what you achieve, it's about what you help others achieve too.

Case Study:
The Value of Mentorship and Networking

Let's take a look at a real-world example that illustrates just how transformative mentorship and networking can be, Chris Gonzalez and his team at Barkly Pets.

When Gonzalez and his co-founders launched Barkly Pets, their vision was clear: to create an on-demand platform for dog walking services that prioritized safety, transparency, and reliability. Like many startups, they had ambition, passion, and a solid product idea. But what they lacked was experience in scaling a tech-enabled service across multiple cities.

That's where mentorship made the difference.

Through SCORE, a nonprofit organization that offers free mentorship to small businesses, the Barkly team connected with experienced business professionals who had been through the trenches. These mentors didn't just pat them on the back or give generic encouragement, they rolled up their sleeves and got involved. They helped the team refine their business model, sharpen their customer acquisition strategies, and optimize their pricing structure.

One of the key takeaways from these mentorship relationships was the importance of managing capital strategically. As the Barkly founders navigated fundraising and expansion into new markets, their mentors provided insight into cash flow management and financial forecasting, areas that often trip up early-stage companies.

But it wasn't just about mentorship, it was also about networking.

Through introductions facilitated by their advisors, the Barkly team was able to secure partnerships with local businesses, meet with potential investors, and even attract experienced talent to join their growing operation. These connections didn't just accelerate their growth, they elevated their brand credibility in a competitive market.

The result? Barkly Pets went from a local startup to a multi-city platform with a scalable model and a loyal user base. And while the founders deserve full credit for their hustle and vision, they're the first to acknowledge that without the guidance, support, and doors opened by their network, their growth would have taken much longer, and cost far more in trial and error.

This case study drives home a powerful truth: mentorship and networking aren't optional extras in entrepreneurship. They're multipliers. They take your skills, your vision, and your momentum, and they amplify it. If you want to go fast, you can go alone. But if you want to go far, find a guide and build your circle.

Final Thought:
Cultivating Your Support System

Entrepreneurship will stretch you. It will test your limits, challenge your assumptions, and sometimes make you feel like you're walking a tightrope without a safety net. But here's the truth: you don't have to do it alone, and you shouldn't.

Behind every successful entrepreneur is a support system. Not just people who cheer from the sidelines, but people who walk with you through the highs and lows. Mentors who've already climbed the mountain and can show you the path. Peers who are grinding it out just like you, offering solidarity and perspective. Team members who believe in your mission and bring their best to the table. And yes, even friends and family who remind you why you started in the first place.

These relationships don't just make the journey more bearable, they make it better. They sharpen your thinking. They call you out when you're slipping. They encourage you when you're stuck. They celebrate when you win. They're your mirrors, your sounding boards, your accountability partners.

But here's the key: support doesn't happen by accident. It must be cultivated.

Be intentional. Reach out. Stay connected. Follow up. Pour into others the same way you want to be poured into. Build a circle where honesty, trust, and mutual growth are the norm.

Because one day you'll hit a wall. You'll face a decision that scares you. You'll question whether you're cut out for this. And when that moment comes, it won't be your business plan or your bank account that pulls you through, it'll be your people.

So build wisely. Invest relationally. And never underestimate the power of community in a world that loves to glorify going it alone.

You don't need a crowd. You need a circle. A tribe. A team.

And once you have that, no challenge feels quite as big, and no dream feels quite as far.

Chapter 10: Time Management and Productivity

You can always earn more money, but you can't earn more time. Every minute you spend is a minute you'll never get back. And in business, how you spend those minutes determines whether you're building something sustainable or just spinning your wheels.

Let me be direct: the way you use your time is the most honest reflection of what matters to you. Your calendar doesn't lie. It shows your values, your discipline, and your focus. If you want to know what someone is really building, don't look at their goals, look at their schedule.

As entrepreneurs, we wear a hundred hats. It's easy to mistake motion for progress, to equate being busy with being productive. But productivity isn't about how much you do, it's about how much of what you do actually moves the needle.

This chapter isn't about working longer hours. It's about working smarter. It's about reclaiming control over your day, protecting your energy, and putting your time where your goals are. Because the truth is, your future is being built in 15-minute blocks right now. And how you manage those blocks will determine everything.

Motion vs. Progress

Entrepreneurs fall into one of the most deceptive traps in business: confusing motion with progress.

You know the feeling. You've been "working" all day, answering emails, reorganizing files, adjusting your website header for the third time this week, and you go to bed exhausted. But when you look at your actual results? Nothing moved. No sales closed. No big project pushed forward. No real traction gained.

That's motion. It feels like work because it is work. But it's not always the right work.

Progress, on the other hand, is intentional. It's the kind of action that moves the needle. It's the sales call you've been avoiding. The pitch you need to refine. The system that, once built, will save you ten hours a week. Progress doesn't always look impressive in the moment, but it compounds. And it creates outcomes.

I had to learn this the hard way. I used to fill my days with motion, staying "busy" so I could avoid the discomfort of doing the work that really mattered. Because progress work is often scarier. It's where the stakes are higher. Where failure feels more personal. But it's also where the growth lives.

If you want to be productive, don't just count your hours, count your results. Ask yourself daily: "Is this task getting me closer to my core objective, or is it just keeping me comfortably occupied?"

Because not all movement is forward movement. And if you want to build something that lasts, you need to stop spinning and start advancing.

My "Non-Negotiables" System

Once I realized that being busy wasn't the same as being effective, I knew I had to change how I approached my days. I needed more than a to-do list, I needed a compass. That's when I developed what I now call my "Non-Negotiables" system.

These aren't just tasks. They're the few key actions that actually move the business forward. The things that, if done consistently, create momentum, build systems, and generate results.

Every morning, before the chaos of the day could take over, I'd sit down and ask myself two questions:

- **What's the one thing I could do today that would make the biggest impact?**

- **What do I need to complete for today to feel like a win?**

The first question keeps me strategic. It forces me to think about leverage, not just labor. It helps me identify the work that builds, client outreach, team development, key decisions, rather than the work that just fills time.

The second question keeps me grounded. It gives me a target I can hit, even on hard days. It turns an overwhelming schedule into a focused plan.

And here's the key: I stopped aiming for perfect days where everything got done. Instead, I aimed for meaningful progress. Every day, a small win. Every day, one step forward.

This system didn't just boost my productivity, it reduced my stress. It gave my days structure, my efforts focus, and my mind peace. I wasn't drowning in busywork anymore. I was leading with intention. And that changed everything.

Time Blocking Changed Everything

For years, I lived by the to-do list. Each morning I'd scribble down a dozen tasks, convinced that sheer hustle would carry me through. But most days ended the same, I'd check off the easy stuff, roll the rest to tomorrow, and collapse into bed feeling like I'd run hard but gone nowhere.

That's when I discovered time blocking, and it changed everything.

Time blocking isn't just about scheduling your day. It's about owning it. It means assigning specific blocks of time on your calendar to specific types of work, treating them like immovable appointments. No more vague intentions. No more multitasking. Just focused, intentional effort.

Here's how I block my time now:
- **Deep Work:** These are my highest-value hours, early in the morning, when my mind is sharpest. I use them for strategy, creative projects, or major decisions. No emails. No interruptions.

- **Admin:** I group all logistical tasks, emails, invoices, scheduling, into a single block. That way, they don't leak into my most productive hours.

- **Meetings:** I stack them back-to-back when possible, so I'm not pulled in and out of flow all day.

- **Recovery:** This might be the most important block of all. Time to move, eat, think, breathe, and reconnect. Without it, everything else suffers.

And here's the surprising part: when I started blocking my time, I actually worked less, but accomplished more. Why? Because I wasn't reacting. I was executing.

Time blocking gave me clarity. It forced me to prioritize. It helped me protect the hours that matter most. It didn't make my schedule rigid, it made it purposeful. And in entrepreneurship, that purpose is everything.

Energy > Time

For years, I tried to manage my time like it was the answer to everything. I optimized my calendar. I tracked every hour. I followed every productivity hack I could find.

But something was still off.

I had the time, I just didn't have the energy.

That's when I had a realization that changed the game: time is only as valuable as the energy you bring to it. A 60-minute block of focused, energized work will outperform five sluggish, distracted hours every time. The real edge? It's not managing time, it's managing energy.

So I made some key shifts.
- **I started prioritizing sleep.** Not just getting more of it, but getting better sleep. I cut back on screens at night, created a wind-down routine, and made rest non-negotiable.

- **I changed how I ate.** I stopped using food as stress relief and started using it as fuel. Lighter lunches. More water. Less sugar. My brain started working better because I stopped weighing it down.

- **I moved my body.** Even short walks or quick workouts gave me a jolt of clarity and stamina. Movement wasn't just for my health, it was for my hustle.

- **I eliminated noise.** During deep work, I shut off notifications, closed extra tabs, and let my phone live in another room. That silence became my superpower.

- **And I got ruthless about boundaries.** I started saying "no" to things, and people, that drained me. Every "no" became a "yes" to higher energy and better focus.

The result? I got more done in less time. With less stress. More clarity. More creativity. More calm.

You don't need more hours in your day. You need more life in your hours. Manage your energy, and you'll find the time takes care of itself.

Tools I Actually Use

Let's be real: there are a million productivity tools out there, apps, systems, templates, planners. It's easy to fall into the trap of thinking the next tool is going to change everything.

But here's what I've learned: **tools don't create discipline, discipline makes the tools work.**

That's why I keep my tech stack simple. I don't need 17 apps. I just need a few that help me stay focused, track what matters, and reflect consistently.
- **Google Calendar** – This is the backbone of my schedule. I don't just use it for meetings. I block time for deep work, planning, workouts, even family time. If it's not on the calendar, it usually doesn't happen.

- **Trello** – This is my command center for project management. Whether I'm launching a product, planning content, or mapping out a business process, Trello helps me visualize the flow and keep tasks moving.

- **Evernote or Notion** – One of these is always open. They're where I capture ideas, map out strategies, journal, and plan. It's my digital brain. When I need to remember something or flesh out a thought, this is where it lives.

- **Pomodoro Timer** – This simple method, 25 minutes of focused work followed by a 5-minute break, has been a game changer. It breaks big tasks into bite-sized sprints and trains my brain to work with urgency and clarity.

- **Weekly Reflection Journal** – Once a week, usually on Sundays, I sit down and answer a few key questions: What were my wins? What drained me? What do I need to adjust? This habit has sharpened my self-awareness and helped me course-correct in real-time.

None of these tools are magic. They don't do the work for you. But when paired with consistent habits and clear priorities, they become powerful allies.

Remember this: the best productivity system is the one you actually use. Keep it simple. Stay consistent. Let the tools support your discipline, not replace it.

Saying "No" Is a Productivity Superpower

One of the most underrated skills in business, and in life, is the ability to say no.

As an entrepreneur, your time is your most valuable asset. And if you don't protect it, everyone else will spend it for you. Clients will overstep boundaries. Vendors will demand unnecessary meetings. Friends and family, with the best intentions, will pull your attention away from the work that actually moves the needle.

You don't owe the world your immediate availability.
- You don't need to respond to every email the moment it hits your inbox.

- You don't have to say yes to every coffee meeting or collaboration request.
- You don't need to explain yourself for setting boundaries.

Every time you say "yes" to something trivial, you're saying "no" to something meaningful. And over time, those tiny compromises cost you clarity, progress, and peace.

Saying "no" doesn't make you rude. It makes you strategic.

It's a sign of focus. Of intention. Of knowing what matters and refusing to let distractions dilute your power.

Here's a quick mindset shift: instead of asking, "Can I fit this in?", ask, "Does this align with my top priorities?" If the answer is no, let it go.

Your calendar should be a reflection of your mission, not a dumping ground for other people's agendas.

Learn to protect it with the same tenacity you protect your profit margins. Because wasted time is far more expensive than you think.

My Sunday Night Ritual

Every Sunday night, like clockwork, I carve out 20 quiet minutes to sit down and look ahead. No TV. No distractions. Just me, my calendar, and a clear mind.

It's one of the simplest habits I've developed, and one of the most powerful.

Here's what I walk through each week:

1. **Top 3 Outcomes**
   I don't ask, "What do I have to get done?" I ask, "What are the three most important outcomes I need to create this week?"
   These aren't tasks, they're results. Things that actually move the business forward. It might be closing a deal, launching a campaign, or making a key hire. If I only accomplished these three things, would I still feel like the week was a win?

2. **Schedule Review**
   Next, I scan my calendar. What's already locked in?
   What meetings, events, or deadlines are coming? I look for gaps, bottle-necks, or double-bookings. Then I ask, "Is this the right use of my time?"
   If not, I adjust.

3. **Delegate and Eliminate**
   Finally, I review my to-do list and ask two questions:
   • What can someone else do better or faster than me? (Delegate it.)
   • What doesn't actually need to be done at all? (Eliminate it.)

This 20-minute ritual helps me start every week with clarity, intention, and control. It removes the mental clutter before it builds. It turns chaos into strategy. And it sets the tone for how I lead, how I show up, and how I execute.

It's not flashy. But it works. Every single time.

Case Study:
Liane Agbi's Productivity Pivot

Liane Agbi, a 34-year-old entrepreneur from Jersey City, transformed both her web design business and personal life by reevaluating her work habits. Initially, her demanding schedule strained her relationship with her husband and led to burnout. Recognizing the unsustainable nature of her routine, Liane implemented three pivotal changes:

1. **Establishing Boundaries:** She set firm work hours, ending her day earlier to ensure quality time with her husband.

2. **Seeking Support:** Liane hired a business coach and a junior developer, which improved workflow and allowed her to focus on strategic growth.

3. **Accountability Partnership:** By involving her husband as an accountability partner, she maintained her commitment to work-life balance.

These adjustments not only revitalized her personal life but also significantly boosted her business, increasing her revenue to $192,000 within a year. Business Insider

Liane's experience underscores the importance of setting boundaries, seeking support, and maintaining accountability in achieving both personal well-being and business success.

Final Thought: Master Time or Stay Stuck

You don't need more time. You need more clarity.

You don't need a new planner. You need a new plan.

Entrepreneurs often chase the illusion of more hours in the day, wishing they could stretch time to meet the demands of business, family, and life. But time isn't your problem. Priority is.

The most successful entrepreneurs I know aren't the ones who run the fastest or grind the longest. They're the ones who treat time like an investment portfolio. Every minute is a resource. Every hour is an asset. And every day is a choice.

They manage their energy with precision. They protect their focus like their business depends on it, because it does. They say no to the urgent so they can say yes to the important.

So the next time you hear yourself say, "I don't have time," stop. Challenge that statement. Reframe it.

Say instead: "I haven't made this a priority."

That small change in language creates a massive shift in responsibility, and power. It puts the ownership back where it belongs: in your hands.

Because the truth is, your future is being built in 15-minute blocks right now.

Not someday. Not when things slow down. Right now.

Choose wisely. Lead intentionally. And remember: time management isn't just about getting more done, it's about becoming the kind of person who knows what's worth doing in the first place.

Chapter 11: Motivation, Focus, and Loneliness

Entrepreneurship is often celebrated as a path of freedom, passion, and purpose. It's the dream of building something that matters, making your own rules, and reaping the rewards of your hustle. And while all of that can be true, there's another side that rarely gets the spotlight, one that's quieter, heavier, and far more common than most realize.

Behind the scenes, many entrepreneurs face a different reality: long hours spent alone, weighty decisions that can't be delegated, and internal battles no one else sees. The mental load is relentless. You're not just managing a business, you're managing expectations, relationships, cash flow, and your own self-doubt, all at the same time.

As your business grows, the number of people who truly understand your world often shrinks. Friends might not relate anymore. Family might not grasp the stress you carry. And team members, though valuable, can't always be your sounding board for everything you're wrestling with internally.

This isolation compounds. It can dull your drive, erode your focus, and quietly chip away at your confidence. You begin to question yourself, not because the business is failing, but because the silence feels so loud.

And in those moments, it's easy to forget the most critical truth: you are the business's most important asset. Protecting your mental health, nurturing your motivation, and building strategies to stay focused and connected isn't indulgent, it's essential. Without you, the business doesn't move. Without your clarity, your energy, your sense of purpose, everything else begins to wobble.

Entrepreneurship isn't just about building a profitable company, it's about building a sustainable life. And that means facing these hidden struggles with intention, honesty, and the right tools to keep going even when no one else sees the full weight of what you carry.

Motivation Isn't Magic

A common myth in entrepreneurship, and life, is that motivation comes first. That you'll wake up inspired, brimming with energy, and then go tackle the hard things. But if you've spent any time in the trenches of building a business, you know the truth: that spark rarely shows up on its own.

Motivation isn't some lightning bolt that strikes the lucky. It's not a magical force reserved for the ultra-driven or the perpetually enthusiastic. It's a byproduct of movement. Action creates momentum. And momentum breeds motivation.

In fact, some of the most productive days you'll ever have will start with zero motivation. You'll feel tired. Unfocused. Overwhelmed. But if you show up anyway, make the call, clean the desk, write the email, fix the issue, something begins to shift. The act of doing ignites the desire to keep doing. And suddenly, what felt impossible an hour ago becomes manageable.

This is where discipline steps in. Not as punishment, but as a tool. Discipline says, "I'm not waiting to feel ready. I'm showing up because this matters." And over time, that consistent action becomes the engine that keeps you moving forward, even when motivation dips.

One practical way to spark this momentum is by setting structure in your day. Clear goals, outlined priorities, and a simple action plan can give you the clarity you need to take the first step. Because often, the hardest part isn't the work, it's starting the work. But once you start, your mindset begins to catch up.

Remember: you don't need to feel inspired to get moving. You just need to move. And once you do, motivation will show up, not as a prerequisite, but as a reward.

Cultivating Focus in a Distracted World

In today's world, your attention is under constant attack. Every ping, buzz, banner, and badge is engineered to pull you away from what matters. And it works. Studies show it takes over 20 minutes to regain full focus after an interruption, even a small one. Multiply that across a day, and you're looking at hours of lost potential.

For entrepreneurs, this isn't just inconvenient, it's costly. Your ability to focus determines your ability to lead, strategize, and execute. Without focus, everything slows down. Decisions get delayed. Creativity dries up. Stress piles on.

That's why cultivating focus has to be a priority. It's not just a productivity hack, it's a leadership skill.

Start with **time-blocking**. This simple habit involves scheduling specific chunks of your day for high-impact tasks: strategic thinking, content creation, deep problem-solving. During these blocks, you protect your attention like it's gold, because it is. No calls. No emails. No multitasking. Just focused, intentional work.

Pair that with **batch processing**, grouping similar tasks together so your brain doesn't have to constantly switch gears. Emails in one block. Admin tasks in another. Creative work in its own space. Each type of task demands different energy. Grouping them reduces cognitive drag and increases efficiency.

Next, set **digital boundaries.** Turn off non-essential notifications. Use "Do Not Disturb" mode during deep work hours. Designate certain times to check messages, don't let messages dictate your time. Consider tools like website blockers or focus apps if you find yourself drifting to social media or news feeds.

Lastly, create a **dedicated workspace**. Even if it's just a corner of a room, design a space that signals "focus mode." Clear your desk. Eliminate clutter. Use headphones if needed. Train your brain to associate that space with deep concentration.

In a distracted world, focus is a form of resistance. It's also a competitive edge. While others are scattered, you can be sharp. While others react, you can create. Focus isn't automatic, but with practice, it becomes a habit that multiplies your results.

Confronting the Reality of Loneliness

Entrepreneurship can be exhilarating, but it can also be isolating, especially as your business grows and your responsibilities increase. While you're surrounded by people, employees, clients, vendors, there's often a profound emotional distance. You're the one steering the ship, making the tough calls, and carrying the weight of both success and failure. And that level of responsibility can feel heavy, even suffocating, when carried alone.

This isn't something many entrepreneurs talk about. We celebrate the wins and downplay the hard days. We smile in meetings, post polished updates, and act like we've got it all figured out. But behind closed doors, loneliness can quietly erode our joy, clarity, and confidence.

It's important to understand: feeling isolated doesn't mean you're doing it wrong. It means you're human. And the good news is, loneliness doesn't have to be permanent. You can build intentional structures of connection that not only reduce the isolation but also enrich your entrepreneurial journey.

Here are a few practical strategies:

- **Engage with Peers:**
  Find other entrepreneurs who are walking a similar path. Regular check-ins, whether casual coffee chats or formal accountability calls, can create space for honest conversations, shared wisdom, and mutual encouragement. Knowing someone else gets it can be a powerful antidote to loneliness.

- **Seek Mentorship:**
  Identify leaders who've been where you are, and are where you want to go. A mentor can offer perspective, challenge your thinking, and remind you that you're not alone. Don't be afraid to reach out. Most successful people are more willing to share their experience than you might think.

- **Join Communities:**
  Whether it's a mastermind group, a business forum, or an industry specific network, get plugged into a group where you're not the only one in the room carrying big dreams and big decisions. These environments

foster both accountability and empathy, two things every entrepreneur needs.

- **Be Vulnerable:**
  This might be the hardest one. But it's also the most powerful. Don't bottle everything up. Share the truth with someone you trust. Let others in, not just to celebrate your highs, but to walk with you through the lows.

Entrepreneurship may start as a solo mission, but it doesn't have to stay that way. Connection is more than a comfort, it's a catalyst. It helps you think clearer, lead stronger, and build something that lasts.

So don't retreat into silence. Reach out. Build your circle. Because even though you carry the vision, you were never meant to carry it alone.

Practical Habits to Sustain Well-being

Staying motivated, focused, and emotionally grounded as an entrepreneur isn't just about willpower, it's about rhythm. The demands of building and leading a business can consume you if you don't actively protect your energy and mindset. That's why it's essential to develop practical habits that create space for clarity, renewal, and connection.

Here are a few habits that can make a measurable difference:

- **Daily Reflection:**
  Begin or end each day with intentional reflection. Take five to ten minutes to journal what went well, what challenged you, and what you learned. This isn't about perfection, it's about perspective. Reflection creates awareness. It turns experience into insight. And over time, it becomes a running record of growth that reminds you how far you've come.

- **Scheduled Downtime:**
  Rest doesn't happen by accident. If it's not on your calendar, it won't happen. Block time for rest the same way you block time for meetings. That might mean family dinners, reading time, workouts, or even just a quiet walk. These pauses aren't a break from productivity, they're what sustain

it. Burnout is a silent killer in entrepreneurship, and rest is the antidote.

- **Regular Check-ins:**
  Every quarter (or at least once a month), take a strategic pause.
  Ask yourself: Am I still aligned with my vision?
  What's fueling me? What's draining me?
  What goals still matter, and which need to be adjusted or let go?
  These check-ins are like recalibrating your GPS.
  They help you navigate through the noise and stay on course.

- **Community Engagement:**
  Isolation breeds stagnation. Connection breeds creativity.
  Make it a point to plug into conversations beyond your business.
  Attend local meetups, join mastermind groups, participate in webinars, or contribute to online communities.
  Sometimes a single conversation can unlock a breakthrough idea or shift your entire perspective.

These habits aren't glamorous, but they are game-changing. They form the scaffolding that holds your mindset, energy, and emotional health in place. And when practiced consistently, they do more than just keep you afloat, they help you thrive.

Because running a business is hard. But running yourself into the ground isn't a requirement. Prioritize your well-being like your success depends on it, because it does.

Case Study: Justin and the Product People Club

Justin, a solo entrepreneur and product developer, noticed a troubling trend, not in his business metrics, but in the conversations he was having behind closed doors. Fellow founders, especially those building alone, consistently voiced the same struggles: staying motivated without a team, maintaining focus without accountability, and, above all, feeling isolated.

The deeper he listened, the clearer the need became. These entrepreneurs didn't just need business strategies, they needed connection. They needed a place where they could show up, be seen, and be supported. So Justin launched the **Product People Club**, a small, paid online community for solo founders who were building product-focused businesses.

This wasn't a generic forum or a free Facebook group, it was intentional, curated, and designed for depth. The community offered weekly check-ins, structured accountability, and peer support rooted in real-world challenges. Justin kept it tight-knit on purpose, knowing that intimacy creates trust, and trust fuels transformation.

The result? The initial cohort sold out almost instantly. A waitlist formed. Members began reporting not just improved motivation and productivity, but emotional relief. They no longer felt like they were on an island. They had a tribe. And that tribe made them braver, bolder, and more consistent.

Justin's success wasn't in building a massive network. It was in creating a **meaningful one.**

His story is a powerful reminder that entrepreneurship doesn't have to be lonely, and that community, when done right, is more than a perk. It's a **lifeline.** Sometimes, the difference between burning out and breaking through isn't a new strategy, it's knowing someone's walking the journey with you.

Final Thought: Leading from Within

Before you can lead others, before you can cast vision, drive results, or scale impact, you have to learn how to lead yourself. And that's not about charisma or control. It's about consistency, clarity, and character. It's about doing the quiet, internal work that no one sees so that you can show up strong when it counts.

Leading from within means checking your mindset daily. It means noticing when self-doubt creeps in, when fatigue whispers "just coast," and when distraction tempts you to escape. It means recognizing that discipline isn't about grinding 24/7, it's about protecting the things that truly matter.

It also means managing your energy like your most valuable asset. Not just physically, but emotionally, mentally, and spiritually. Because the version of you that shows up tired, scattered, and reactive won't build the business you dream of. But the version of you that's centered, focused, and grounded, that person can do just about anything.

And here's the deeper truth: the business you're building will only grow to the level that you do. Your capacity to lead is your company's ceiling. Your clarity becomes your team's confidence. Your consistency becomes their culture.

So show up early for yourself. Build habits that feed your strength. Create space for your soul. Surround yourself with people who sharpen you.

Because entrepreneurship isn't just about creating wealth or solving problems. It's about becoming someone who can carry the weight of a dream, and still walk with joy, purpose, and peace.

Lead yourself first. And everything else will follow.

Chapter 12: Building a Team That Builds the Business

Every successful entrepreneur eventually hits the same realization: you can't do it all alone. No matter how sharp your skills, how relentless your drive, or how powerful your vision, there's a ceiling you'll hit if everything depends on you. That's when building a team stops being optional, and starts being essential.

But here's the key: it's not just about hiring bodies. It's about building alignment. It's about surrounding yourself with people who don't just clock in, they buy in. People who see the mission, carry the vision, and make the company stronger because they're part of it.

A high-performing team isn't just a support system, it's a force multiplier. It allows you to delegate with confidence, scale with sustainability, and lead with clarity. And when done right, it becomes one of your greatest competitive advantages.

But great teams don't happen by accident. They're built with intentionality. They require clarity, structure, and leadership. They require you to shift from being the doer to being the builder, from the one who handles everything to the one who empowers others to take ownership.

This chapter isn't just about staffing up. It's about leveling up. Because the team you build will ultimately determine the business you're able to grow.

Transitioning from "Doer" to "Builder"

Every entrepreneur begins as a doer. In the early days, it's all hands on deck, making the sales, answering the emails, tracking the expenses, ordering supplies, updating the website, even sweeping the floors. It's a necessary phase. It teaches you the ins and outs of your business. It builds grit. It builds understanding. It builds appreciation.

But at some point, hustle becomes a handicap.

If your business only works when you're working, you haven't built a business, you've built a job. And no matter how passionate or capable you are, that model isn't sustainable. Eventually, it burns you out or boxes you in.

The real shift, the one that takes you from self-employed to CEO, comes when you stop asking, "How can I get this done?" and start asking, "Who can do this better than me?"

That's when the game changes.

Delegation isn't about dumping tasks. It's about designing your company to scale. It's about trusting others to carry parts of the mission. It's about recognizing that your highest value doesn't come from doing everything, it comes from focusing on what only you can do.

When you build systems, empower people, and let go of control in the right places, you free yourself to lead. To think. To innovate. To grow.

And in doing so, you give your business room to breathe, and the structure to thrive.

The Right Team Outperforms the Right Idea

You can have the most innovative product, the flashiest brand, or the boldest vision, but if the people behind it can't execute, it won't matter. Ideas are important, but execution is everything. And execution lives and dies with your team.

A mediocre idea in the hands of a high-performing, values-aligned team can become something extraordinary. They'll adapt it. Refine it. Bring it to life in ways you never imagined. On the flip side, even the best idea can fall apart when it's surrounded by drama, miscommunication, ego, or apathy.

That's why your team isn't just a support system, it's your multiplier.
People problems are the silent killers of momentum. One disengaged employee can drain morale. One toxic hire can shift the culture. One unclear role can create bottlenecks that ripple through the entire organization. And often, these problems don't show up in obvious ways. They show up in missed deadlines, vague excuses, and the slow erosion of trust and energy.

That's why your hiring philosophy matters.

Hire slowly. Take your time. Look beyond the resume. Assess their mindset, their values, their fit. Are they coachable? Do they take ownership? Can they think beyond their job description?

Fire quickly. If someone is clearly misaligned, no matter how talented they are, don't drag it out. Culture is too important. Energy is too precious. One wrong fit kept too long will cost more than a tough conversation today.

And most importantly, protect your culture like it's your competitive edge, because it is. Your culture is what people feel when they walk into your business. It's what keeps your best people around. It's what turns teams into families and tasks into missions.

Build the right team, and you can turn almost any idea into a win. Let the wrong team linger, and no idea will ever be enough.

Equity Isn't Always the Answer

When you're building a business, especially in the early days, it can be tempting to offer equity to anyone willing to share the load. You might feel overwhelmed, out of your depth, or eager to secure loyalty. And on the surface, offering a slice of the pie seems like a smart way to align incentives and show appreciation.

But here's the truth: equity is expensive. It's not just a percentage of your profits, it's a percentage of your control, your decision-making, and your future.

Not every contributor needs to be a co-owner. In fact, many people don't want that kind of pressure or long-term responsibility. What they want is clarity, respect, compensation, and the opportunity to do meaningful work.

Take Christy, for example. She manages one of my businesses and does it with excellence. She leads teams, solves problems, drives results, and treats the company like it's her own. But she doesn't have equity, and she doesn't need it to care deeply. What she does have is autonomy, trust, and a compensation structure that rewards her performance. That alignment is more powerful than ownership for many roles.

Use equity with intention. Don't hand it out as a bribe or a Band-Aid for fear or burnout. Reserve it for the rare few who are truly irreplaceable, those whose unique contribution and alignment with your mission make them essential to the long-term vision.

If you're trying to build a team, consider profit-sharing, performance bonuses, or tiered incentives before giving away a piece of the business. Because once you give equity, you can't take it back without consequences.

Equity should be a strategic decision, not an emotional one. When used wisely, it can supercharge your business. When used loosely, it can dilute everything you've worked so hard to build.

Hiring for Mindset Over Skill Set

When it comes to building a winning team, technical skills matter, but mindset matters more. You can train someone to use your CRM. You can teach processes, systems, and platforms. But what you can't teach is hunger. Drive. Grit. Initiative.

That's why when I hire, I look beyond the résumé. I'm less interested in where someone went to school or how many certifications they've stacked. What I want to know is how they think. How they respond under pressure. How they show up when no one's watching.
Here's what I'm really looking for:

- **Ownership Mentality:**

Do they take responsibility for their outcomes, or do they make excuses? Do they treat problems like someone else's fault, or do they step up and solve them? People who own their work create results, period.

- **Critical Thinking:**
  Can they think for themselves, or do they need hand-holding for every task? The best team members bring ideas, not just execution. They anticipate roadblocks, offer solutions, and don't wait to be told what to do.

- **Coachability:**
  Are they teachable? Can they receive feedback without getting defensive? In a fast-moving business, growth requires humility. The people who evolve fastest are the ones who don't let their ego block their development.

- **Cultural Fit:**
  Do they align with the mission and values of the business? You can have a rockstar performer who creates chaos because they don't share the culture. That's a net loss. I'd rather hire someone who's slightly less experienced but deeply aligned with who we are and where we're going.

I've seen firsthand what happens when you hire solely for skill, it often backfires. Yes, they can do the job, but can they grow with the role? Can they lead others? Can they innovate when the playbook runs out?

Hiring for mindset ensures that the people you bring on are resilient, agile, and engaged. They won't just survive change, they'll thrive in it. They won't just do the work, they'll elevate it.

So when you're evaluating candidates, don't just ask, "Can they do this job today?" Ask, "Will they grow into who we need tomorrow?" Because that's how you build a team that scales with your vision.

Investing in Training and Development

Hiring someone is just the starting line, not the finish. The real transformation happens when you commit to developing your team after they're on board. Great businesses aren't built by great hires alone, they're built by great training, intentional development, and leadership that multiplies capability.

Too many entrepreneurs make the mistake of assuming that because someone was impressive in an interview, they'll automatically deliver results. But no one walks into your company already knowing how you do things. Even the most talented people need direction, context, and support to thrive.

Training your team well isn't just about teaching them what to do. It's about showing them why it matters. The "how" gives them the task. The "why" gives them the ownership.

When you share the purpose behind the process, why this client interaction matters, why accuracy in this report makes a difference, why the system exists the way it does, you're not just transferring information. You're transferring vision. That clarity creates alignment, and alignment creates momentum.

But development doesn't stop with onboarding. You have to keep investing in your people. That means:

- Regular feedback loops that help them improve.
- Ongoing learning opportunities, like courses, workshops, or peer coaching.
- Clear paths for growth so they can see a future with you.
- Space to take initiative, make decisions, and even make mistakes without fear.

Yes, this takes time. Yes, it takes patience. But the payoff is exponential. Because every hour you spend developing your team is an hour you're buying back for yourself in the future. When your team can think, lead, and solve without you, you're no longer a bottleneck, you're a builder of leaders.

And that's when real freedom starts.

Don't just build a team that follows instructions. Build a team that understands the mission, makes smart decisions, and leads alongside you. That's how you scale not just your business, but your impact.

Cultivating a Purposeful Culture

Culture isn't something you write once and stick on the wall. It's something you live, breathe, and reinforce every single day. It's not defined by the posters in your conference room, it's defined by how your team behaves when no one's watching. How they respond under pressure. How they treat each other. How they show up for the mission.

As a leader, you don't just influence the culture, you are the culture. Your words, your tone, your habits, they all set the standard. If you're scattered, the team will be chaotic. If you value integrity, they'll mirror that too. Culture trickles down from the top, whether you intend it to or not.

A strong, purposeful culture isn't built on perks or slogans. It's built on principles. And when those principles are clear, consistent, and embodied by leadership, they become contagious.

Here's what that looks like in practice:

- **Take Ownership:**
  Your team doesn't pass the buck. They step up, take initiative, and hold themselves accountable for outcomes, not just activities. When something goes wrong, the question is never, "Whose fault is this?" It's, "What can we learn and how can we fix it?"

- **Communicate Openly:**
  Healthy teams don't hide problems, they surface them early. They don't sugarcoat feedback, they offer it with care. Open communication builds trust, and trust accelerates performance.

- **Support Each Other:**
  In great cultures, people aren't stepping on each other to climb the ladder, they're lifting each other up. Wins are shared. Struggles are carried together. You don't just have coworkers, you have teammates.

- **Celebrate Successes:**
  Recognition isn't a nice-to-have, it's a must. People do more of what gets noticed. Whether it's a record-breaking sale or a small behind-the-scenes

win, make it a point to call it out. Momentum is built through celebration.

- **Learn from Mistakes:**
  In high-trust cultures, failure isn't fatal, it's feedback. Your team won't innovate unless they feel safe taking smart risks. Normalize learning out loud. When someone stumbles, use it as a teaching moment, not a trigger for shame.

When you intentionally shape your culture around these values, you'll find that your business starts to attract a different kind of person, driven, self-aware, collaborative, and aligned. And once those people are in the room, your business doesn't just grow. It multiplies.

Because in the long run, it's not your product, your price, or your marketing that sustains your company.

It's your culture. Always.

Case Study:
Ethos Farm's Team-Centric Growth

Sally Alington's journey with Ethos Farm is a textbook example of how building a strong, values-driven team can become a company's greatest competitive advantage.

After leaving her corporate role in 2017, Alington launched Ethos Farm, a customer service training consultancy aimed at improving passenger experiences in airports and travel hubs. It was a bold move into entrepreneurship, and like many founders, she was stepping into uncertainty with more grit than guarantees.

From day one, Alington prioritized people. While many startups fixate solely on growth hacks and product-market fit, she focused on building an internal culture of care, communication, and accountability. She believed that when employees feel valued, heard, and supported, they show up differently, for each other and for the customer.

That philosophy paid off in a big way.

Ethos Farm didn't just grow, it soared. Within a few short years, the company was generating £24.9 million in revenue and employing over 1,300 staff. The secret? A leadership approach that put team engagement at the center of strategy. Alington didn't just hire people, she empowered them. She built systems that encouraged ownership, celebrated contribution, and created clarity around the mission.

But perhaps the most powerful proof of her leadership came not in the numbers, but in a moment of crisis.

When Alington's husband was diagnosed with cancer, she was forced to step back from the day-to-day. It was one of the hardest seasons of her life. And in that moment, the true strength of her team was revealed. They rallied. They stepped up. They didn't just keep the business afloat, they kept it growing. Because they weren't just employees, they were invested. In the mission. In each other. In her.

That's what team-driven leadership looks like.

Sally Alington's story is more than inspiring, it's instructive. It reminds us that when you build a business on culture, values, and trust, you don't just build a company that grows. You build one that endures. Through personal challenges. Through market shifts. Through anything.

Because at the end of the day, your people aren't just your workforce. They're your greatest asset, your brand ambassadors, and often, your safety net.

Final Thought: Your Team Is Your Legacy

Building a team isn't just a practical necessity, it's a legacy-defining decision. Every hire, every conversation, every cultural value you reinforce becomes part of the DNA of your business. And long after the spreadsheets are archived and the logos evolve, it's the people you empowered who will carry your vision forward.

Great leaders don't just delegate tasks, they develop people. They look beyond resumes and titles, and instead invest in potential, character, and alignment. They don't just build teams to help them get through the week, they build teams to shape what their business becomes in the next decade.

The truth is, your business will only grow as fast as your people do. So ask yourself:

- Are you building a team of order-takers or problem-solvers?
- Are you developing followers or future leaders?
- Are you surrounding yourself with people who challenge you, complement you, and elevate your mission?

Legacy isn't just about what you leave behind, it's about what you leave in motion.

So build with intention. Lead with clarity. And never forget that the team you cultivate today is the echo of your leadership tomorrow.

Because in the end, your business might bear your name, but it's your team that carries its heartbeat. Nurture that, and you won't just build a company, you'll build a legacy worth remembering.

Chapter 13: Decision Making Under Pressure

Entrepreneurs are decision-makers by nature. Every day brings a barrage of choices, strategic hires, pricing models, marketing channels, product features, customer problems, financial priorities. Some decisions are monumental, others are minute, but together they create a nonstop current of mental demands.

This unrelenting pace can lead to a very real and dangerous condition: **decision fatigue.**

Decision fatigue is more than just feeling tired. It's the gradual erosion of your ability to make quality decisions due to cognitive overload. When your brain is forced to make hundreds of choices a day, even small ones, like what to eat, which meeting to attend, or which message to reply to, it starts to lose its sharpness. You get reactive instead of reflective. You lean toward the easiest option, not the best one. Or worse, you avoid deciding at all.

And here's the danger: the higher the stakes, the more likely decision fatigue will lead to costly mistakes. That means a business owner under stress might delay a necessary hire, overcommit resources, ignore warning signs, or say yes when they should say no.

That's why recognizing decision fatigue isn't just helpful, it's essential. Your ability to lead, grow, and stay ahead hinges on staying clear, calm, and confident under pressure.

Mitigating this fatigue requires more than rest. It requires systems. Routines. Support. And most of all, a mindset that understands the brain is a limited resource, and smart leaders protect it like their most valuable asset.

Preparation Over Panic

When the pressure is on and the clock is ticking, the best leaders don't guess, they prepare. Effective decision-making in high-stakes moments doesn't require nerves of steel or superhuman instincts. It requires a solid process. And that process starts long before the crisis ever arrives.

Preparation isn't about predicting every challenge, it's about equipping yourself with a mental playbook that can guide you through uncertainty with clarity and confidence. Here's how I approach it:

- **Assess the Worst-Case Scenario:** When emotions run high, your brain tends to catastrophize. But actually naming the worst-case scenario does two things: it shrinks the fear, and it allows you to plan around it. If you can live with the worst, you can act with courage. And if the worst is unacceptable, you know where to fortify.

- **Evaluate the Full Cost:** Every decision carries a cost, and it's not always financial. There are emotional costs, like stress, distraction, and burnout. There are relational costs, team morale, trust, customer satisfaction. When you factor in all dimensions, your decisions get smarter and more sustainable.

- **Allow for Flexibility:** Not every choice is a forever decision. Some paths can be reversed or refined. Ask, "Can I pivot if this doesn't work?" If the answer is yes, the risk becomes more manageable, and so does the pressure.

- **Align With Core Values:** In moments of stress, shortcuts can be tempting. But the leaders who last are the ones who anchor their decisions in values. When you're clear on what matters most, integrity, excellence, impact, you avoid regret and stay consistent, even in chaos.

Preparation is what keeps panic at bay. It transforms pressure into performance, fear into focus, and complexity into clarity.

The 40/70 Rule

General Colin Powell, a celebrated military leader and statesman, introduced a powerful concept that every entrepreneur should internalize: the 40/70 Rule. His advice? Never make a decision with less than 40% of the information you need, but don't wait for more than 70%.

In business, the pressure to make the "right" choice can be paralyzing. Entrepreneurs often believe they need perfect data, complete certainty, and total alignment before pulling the trigger. But in reality, the perfect moment rarely arrives. Waiting too long doesn't protect you, it costs you.

The 40/70 rule creates a healthy decision-making window. Here's how it breaks down:

- **Less than 40%? It's a guess.** If you don't have enough insight, data, or context, you're flying blind. Decisions made from this place are reactionary and often reckless. You need a solid foundation to move with purpose.

- **More than 70%? It's a delay.** By the time you have 90 or 100% certainty, the opportunity may have passed. Competitors move faster. Momentum stalls. You start mistaking research for progress and due diligence for avoidance.

This rule forces action while still honoring preparation. It recognizes that in leadership, your job isn't to be perfect, it's to move. To make the best call you can with what you know, and trust yourself to adjust as needed.

For me, this principle has become a gut-check. When I'm staring down a tough call, I ask:

- Do I have enough context to understand the core issue?
- Am I just stalling because I'm afraid of being wrong?
- What happens if I wait too long?

More often than not, I find myself in the 40–70% zone. And when I act within that range, I move faster, stay more agile, and keep my business from stagnating.

The 40/70 rule reminds us that good leadership isn't about perfection, it's about progress. It's not about avoiding mistakes, it's about learning fast, correcting faster, and staying in motion.

The Role of Instinct

Instinct is often misunderstood in business. Some dismiss it as guesswork or emotion-driven impulse, but real instinct, the kind that can guide high-stakes decisions, is anything but random. It's the silent wisdom that forms when experience, repetition, and reflection meet.

Every sales call you've made, every deal you've closed, every mistake you've learned from, they all leave a mark. Over time, those experiences become internalized. You start to recognize patterns faster. You pick up on tone shifts in conversations. You feel when a deal is off before you can articulate why. That's instinct at work.

In pressure-filled situations, instinct becomes an essential decision-making tool. It fills in the gaps when data is incomplete. It offers direction when there's no time for long deliberation. But here's the key: the best instincts are informed. They're rooted in experience, not ego.

I've learned to trust my gut, but only after doing the work. Reading the reports. Learning the hard lessons. Watching trends. Listening more than I speak. That preparation gives my instincts credibility. It's not a wild hunch, it's a fast calculation my brain has been trained to make.

But instinct isn't infallible. It should be tested, cross-checked, and balanced with logic. It's a voice in the room, not the only one.

When I've made my best decisions under pressure, instinct played a role. It nudged me when the numbers looked right but the deal felt wrong. It gave me confidence when the opportunity was unclear but the alignment was obvious. It helped me move when hesitation could have cost everything.

So yes, lean into your instinct, but earn the right to trust it. Train it. Feed it. Strengthen it through real work and honest reflection. Because in business, the faster you can make high-quality decisions, the more ground you'll cover, and your instinct is one of the best tools you'll ever sharpen.

Tools for Decision-Making Under Pressure

In high-stakes moments, your ability to make clear, confident decisions can make or break your business. And while instinct and experience play major roles, having practical tools at your disposal can help you stay grounded and effective when the pressure mounts. Here are four essential tools I use when decisions need to be made fast, and made well:

1. **Controlled Breathing:**

   It sounds simple, but it's powerful. When you're under pressure, your body enters a stress response, your heart rate spikes, your breathing shortens, and your mind can start racing. Taking just 30 seconds for deep, controlled breathing activates your parasympathetic nervous system. It calms you down, clears mental fog, and shifts your brain from reactive to reflective. Before you make a call, send an email, or walk into a tough meeting, breathe. The pause often brings clarity.

2. **Scenario Planning:**

   One of the best ways to get out of fear and into clarity is to ask: "What's the best-case scenario? What's the worst? What's most likely?" By mapping out these three options, you reduce the emotional weight of the decision. Suddenly, the fear of the unknown has parameters. It becomes a problem to solve, not a panic to survive. And even if the worst happens, you're not blindsided, you're prepared.

3. **Consultation:**

   You don't have to go it alone. Some of the wisest decisions I've made came after a quick call to a trusted mentor or peer. Not to outsource the decision, but to gain perspective. A five-minute conversation can reveal blind spots, offer fresh insights, or simply confirm what you already suspected. Build a personal board of advisors, people you respect, who understand your values, and who aren't afraid to tell you the hard truth.

4. Commitment:

Wavering kills momentum. Once you've made a thoughtful decision, based on values, data, instinct, or advice, commit to it. Indecision drains energy and confuses your team. That doesn't mean you ignore new information or resist change. But it does mean you move forward with purpose. Adjust if needed, but don't stall in fear. The most effective leaders make decisions, own them, and course-correct as necessary.

In pressure moments, your brain wants to react. These tools help you respond, with calm, clarity, and conviction. They won't eliminate risk, but they will increase your readiness. And that's what separates reactive entrepreneurs from strategic leaders.

Case Study:
Dan Price and Gravity Payments

In 2015, Dan Price, the founder and CEO of Gravity Payments, made a decision that stunned the business world. Amid a climate of rising income inequality and stagnant wages, he announced that every employee at his company would earn a minimum salary of $70,000, and that he would slash his own salary from $1.1 million down to that same number to make it happen.

It wasn't a decision made lightly. Price faced enormous pressure. Financial analysts warned the move could bankrupt the company. Business owners and pundits criticized him for what they saw as naive, unsustainable generosity. Even some of his own clients threatened to leave. But Price wasn't reacting to trends or critics, he was responding to a deeper conviction.

He had read a study showing that emotional well-being plateaued after an individual earns about $70,000 per year. That sparked a question: what if his company's culture, retention, and performance could be dramatically improved not by squeezing more out of people, but by investing more into them?

Despite the backlash, Price moved forward. Over time, the results spoke for themselves.

Productivity rose. Employee engagement soared. Turnover rates plummeted. More impressively, the company's revenue doubled, and the number of new customers skyrocketed. Gravity Payments wasn't just surviving, it was thriving. Employees were buying homes, starting families, and paying off debt. Their loyalty and motivation became the company's greatest competitive advantage.

Dan Price's decision became a case study in leadership under pressure. It demonstrated what can happen when values are prioritized over optics, and when courage is paired with conviction. His move may not be replicable in every business, but the principle behind it is universal: the best decisions, especially in moments of pressure, are the ones rooted in purpose, not panic.

This case highlights an essential truth for entrepreneurs: the pressure to conform will always be there. But when your decisions align with your core values and long-term vision, you don't just lead a business, you lead a movement.

Final Thought: The Essence of Leadership

True leadership isn't forged in calm, it's refined in crisis. It's not about making perfect decisions, but about making purposeful ones when the pressure is highest and the stakes are real. What defines great leaders isn't that they always know what to do, but that they're willing to act with courage, clarity, and conviction, especially when others hesitate.

Pressure will always be part of the entrepreneurial journey. There will be moments when the data is incomplete, the clock is ticking, and the consequences are real. In those moments, your preparation becomes your lifeline. Your experience becomes your compass. Your values become your guide.

By building systems for decision-making, practicing scenario planning, seeking trusted input, and refining your instincts through experience, you prepare yourself to move with purpose, not panic. And when you root your decisions in integrity and alignment with your long-term vision, you lead with confidence, even when outcomes aren't guaranteed.

Leadership isn't about having every answer. It's about standing tall in the moment of truth and saying, "Here's where we're going, and here's why."

That kind of leadership doesn't just navigate pressure, it transforms it into progress.

Chapter 14: Legacy and Long-Term Vision

At some point in your entrepreneurial journey, the metrics that once drove you, revenue, growth, survival, start to shift. You build your business. You prove the model. You hit the financial goals you once thought were out of reach. And then, a deeper question begins to rise: **What now?**

That's the moment when the conversation moves from success to **significance**.

Legacy is where vision meets impact. It's not just about how much money you accumulate, or how many businesses you launch, it's about what endures when you're no longer in the room. It's about what you stand for, what you build into others, and what you leave behind in people's hearts, habits, and horizons.

Your legacy isn't the business itself. It's how that business shaped lives. It's the culture you created, the leaders you developed, the community you served, and the standard you set. It's your fingerprints on people's futures, not just your name on the door.

And here's the powerful truth: legacy isn't something you leave. **It's something you build, daily.**

Every decision, every investment in people, every value-driven choice is a brick in the foundation of something that can outlive you. When you start thinking that way, your goals stretch further. Your patience grows. Your leadership deepens.

You stop chasing quick wins, and start building enduring ones. You stop trying to look successful, and start trying to **be** significant.

Legacy isn't about ego. It's about stewardship. It's about understanding that your success was never just about you, it was about what you could do for others because of it.

And that shift? That's when your work begins to matter most.

Why Vision Matters

In the whirlwind of entrepreneurship, it's easy to get consumed by the immediate, deadlines, client needs, daily operations. But without a long-term vision, all that activity can become motion without meaning.

Vision is what keeps you grounded in purpose when your calendar is full and your energy is stretched thin. It's what gives your "yes" power and your "no" clarity. It helps you filter opportunities through a lens of purpose, not just profit.

A clear vision does more than guide decisions, it **shapes culture**, **sets expectations**, and **builds resilience**. When you know where you're headed, it becomes easier to withstand setbacks because you're not just fighting for the moment, you're building for the future.

And vision isn't about fantasy. It's not wishful thinking. It's strategic, directional, and deeply personal. A good vision statement isn't just aspirational, it's operational. It defines where you're going and how you plan to get there. It aligns your team, clarifies your priorities, and serves as a compass when you're navigating uncertainty.

Without vision, you react. With vision, you lead.

When your vision is clear, you stop chasing everything that glitters and start investing in what truly grows. You build with patience, lead with purpose, and endure with conviction, because you're not just working a plan, **you're living out a mission**.

From Success to Significance

Every entrepreneur begins with a hunger for success. You hustle to pay the bills, prove your idea, and validate your worth in a crowded market. In those early days, success is survival, it's about traction, profit, and staying in the game.

But as the wins start to stack up and the foundation of your business gets stronger, a new question starts to surface, one that has nothing to do with revenue and everything to do with meaning: **What am I really building here?**

This is the tipping point, the moment you begin to shift from success to significance.

Success is hitting your goals. Significance is creating value that outlasts you.

Success fills your bank account. Significance fills your soul.

That's when the deeper questions emerge:

- What kind of leader do I want to be?
- What kind of culture am I creating?
- How do I treat people, not just when business is booming, but when it's hard?
- What kind of legacy am I leaving in the lives of my employees, my customers, my family?

And perhaps the most pivotal of all: **Will what I'm building still matter when I'm no longer the one running it?**

When you start living from those answers, your decisions change. You stop making choices purely for short-term gains and start making moves that reflect your core values. You build with intention, lead with integrity, and give your best not just to succeed, but to serve, to impact, and to inspire.

This is where true fulfillment lives. In knowing that your work isn't just profitable, it's purposeful.

Building for the Long Game

Building something that truly lasts, something that doesn't just flash for a season but endures for generations, requires a different mindset. It's not just about maximizing profit today. It's about making decisions with tomorrow in mind. It's about laying a foundation strong enough to carry weight for years to come. Here's how you do that:

1. **Clarify Your Core Values.**

   Before you can lead others or scale a business, you need to know what you stand for. What are your non-negotiables? What will you fight for, even when it costs you something? These values become your filter. They shape your hiring, your culture, your customer experience, and your decision-making. When you know your values, you stop chasing every opportunity, and start building with consistency and conviction.

2. **Think in Decades, Not Just Days.**

   Short-term goals are important, but long-term vision is what keeps you steady. Ask yourself: What do I want this company, this brand, this impact to look like in 10, 20, even 50 years? How do the choices I make today shape that vision? Legacy builders don't just think about this quarter, they think about the next generation.

3. **Invest in People.**

   Systems scale a business, but people scale a legacy. Teach what you know. Empower your team. Share the lessons, not just the tasks. When you mentor someone, whether it's an employee, a peer, or a future leader, you're planting seeds that will bear fruit long after you're gone. That's how your work multiplies: through others who carry the mission forward.

4. **Protect Your Integrity.**

   There will be shortcuts. Fast wins. Shiny offers. But your reputation, your name, is the one thing you can't afford to lose. Integrity is the currency of lasting influence. Make decisions you're proud of, even when no one's watching. Say what you mean. Keep your word. Lead with honor. Because when the spotlight fades, integrity is what remains.

5. **Balance Ambition With Presence.**

   Build big, but don't miss the moments that matter. Be home for dinner. Go to the games. Celebrate the small stuff. Don't trade your life away for a dream that leaves you empty. Success isn't just hitting your goals; it's being fully present while you do. Live the kind of life you won't regret when you look back on it.

Case Study: Patagonia

When you think of a company that embodies long-term vision and values-driven leadership, Patagonia stands out as a shining example. Founded by Yvon Chouinard, an avid climber and environmentalist, Patagonia wasn't just created to sell outdoor gear, it was built to change how business interacts with the planet.

From the beginning, Chouinard operated with a different set of priorities. He didn't want growth at any cost. He wanted responsibility. Sustainability. Impact. Patagonia pioneered the use of recycled materials, openly shared its supply chain practices, and even ran marketing campaigns urging customers to *not* buy products they didn't need. That wasn't a gimmick, it was a principle. A stand.

But the company's most radical decision came in 2022, when Chouinard transferred ownership of Patagonia, valued at approximately $3 billion, not to his children, but to a trust and a nonprofit dedicated to fighting climate change. Instead of cashing out, he cashed in on his values. Every dollar not reinvested in the business now goes toward protecting the environment.

That's not just leadership. That's legacy.

Patagonia's story proves that you can build a wildly successful business *and* stay deeply aligned with your principles. You can grow profit *and* purpose. You can play the long game, and win.

For entrepreneurs, this case study is more than inspirational. It's instructional. It reminds us that legacy isn't just about what you leave behind, it's about how you show up every day while you're here. Chouinard didn't wait until the end to think about his legacy. He baked it into every decision, every policy, every product, and every pivot.

And the result? A company that customers trust, employees love, and the world respects.

Final Thought: Build What Matters

At the end of the day, success is empty if it doesn't mean something.

You weren't made just to chase metrics. You were made to create meaning. To build something that reflects your values, serves others, and stands the test of time, not just in terms of profit, but in terms of purpose.

Legacy doesn't begin the day you retire or the moment your name is etched on a building. It begins the moment you decide to build with intention. When you choose to lead with integrity, treat people well, solve real problems, and invest your time in things that outlast you.

So ask yourself: what do I want my work to stand for? What do I want people to remember when they hear my name, not just in the business world, but in my family, my community, and my circle of influence?

The goal isn't just to make money. It's to make meaning. The goal isn't just to succeed. It's to matter.

So build the business, yes. Scale it. Grow it. But build your life with just as much care. Prioritize relationships. Leave room for rest. Stay grounded in your purpose. And keep the big picture in view.

Because the most powerful legacy you can leave isn't a number in a bank account. It's a business that lifted people, a life that inspired others, and a ripple effect of impact that continues long after you're gone.

That's legacy. And it starts right now, with the vision you cast, the decisions you make, and the way you choose to build what matters most.

Conclusion: The Mindset That Builds a Legacy

You've reached the final chapter, but let's be clear, this isn't the end. It's the starting line. A reset. A charge. A call to build something bolder, deeper, and more meaningful than just another business.

Because if you've made it this far, you've seen it: the most important asset in entrepreneurship isn't your business model or your marketing strategy, it's your mindset.

Your mindset is the filter through which you see problems, people, and possibility. It's the story you tell yourself when things fall apart, and the fuel that keeps you moving when no one's watching. It's the quiet strength behind every bold decision, the inner compass that helps you lead with clarity, and the resilience that keeps you in the game when others quit.

You've learned how to challenge your beliefs, sharpen your focus, and reset your relationship with failure. You've seen how confidence is built, how fear is faced, how relationships are leveraged, and how long-term vision creates lasting impact. You've been equipped, not just with insight, but with tools.

Now, it's on you.

This book can't hustle for you. It won't make the pitch or write the check. It can't answer hard questions in a boardroom or calm your nerves before a big move. But it can do something even more important, it can remind you, in your toughest moments, who you are and what you're capable of.

You are not just an entrepreneur. You are a builder. A problem-solver. A leader. A visionary. And if you choose to apply this mindset daily, in your thoughts, your words, your work, and your decisions, you won't just build a successful business.

You'll build a meaningful life.

One that outlives the setbacks. One that lifts others. One that becomes your legacy.

So go back to the beginning if you need to. Re-read the chapters that hit hardest. Highlight what sparked something in you. Recommit. Rebuild. Restart.

But don't stay stuck.

Do the work. Trust the process. Build with vision. Lead with purpose. And when the time comes to look back on what you created, you won't just see a business, you'll see a story worth telling.

That's the mindset that builds a legacy.

And it starts with you.

What Comes Next

This isn't just a book, it's a blueprint for transformation. But transformation doesn't happen in a single moment. It happens in the decisions you make after the moment passes.

So what comes next?

Revisit the chapters that hit hardest. Go back to the sections that challenged you, convicted you, or awakened something deep inside. Read them again, not as a passive reader, but as a builder with a mission. This time, ask, "What does this mean for me, right now?"

Reread the parts that stirred something in you. The truth that resonates is usually the truth you need most. Sit with it. Reflect on it. Let it sink past the surface. Then let it move you into action.

Write down what you'll do differently, tomorrow, next week, next year.

Clarity is power, but clarity without action is wasted potential. Get specific. What habit will you start? What conversation will you have? What fear will you face? What system will you implement? Don't just think it, write it. Then do it.

Share this book with someone who's in the fight with you. Growth is multiplied when it's shared. Pass it to a peer, a teammate, a spouse, or a fellow entrepreneur. Talk about it. Challenge each other. Hold each other accountable. We rise faster when we rise together.

Build your community. Entrepreneurship is hard enough, don't do it alone. Surround yourself with people who believe in your vision, push you to grow, and remind you of your strength when you forget. Whether it's a mastermind, a mentor, or a group text with trusted friends, build your circle with intention.

Keep growing. Keep pushing. Don't settle. Don't coast. The leader your vision requires is still becoming. So keep learning. Keep refining. Keep showing up. Because every time you choose growth over comfort, clarity over chaos, and purpose over panic, you're getting closer to the legacy you're meant to leave.

The journey doesn't end here. It begins again, stronger, wiser, and more committed than ever.

And you're ready for it.

My Final Encouragement

You are not behind. You are not broken. You are becoming.

It's easy to look around and feel like you should be further along. To compare your chapter two to someone else's chapter twenty. To see their wins and wonder if you've missed your chance. But hear me clearly, *you haven't.*

You are not late. You are not lacking. You are learning. Evolving. Stepping into the next version of yourself one courageous choice at a time.

Everything you need is inside you. The clarity. The grit. The resourcefulness.

The creativity. The wisdom. It may need refining, it may need coaching, it may need time, but it's there. You just have to trust it. Believe in it. And act like it.

You can build a business that lasts. One that reflects your values, your vision, and your voice. You can create wealth, real, meaningful wealth, without selling out your soul, your health, or your relationships. You can live a life that feels like yours. Not just impressive on the outside, but deeply fulfilling on the inside.

But none of that happens by accident. It happens when you decide, *really decide*, to own your mindset. To take responsibility for your growth. To lead yourself with discipline, integrity, and courage, even when it's hard.

And if that sounds overwhelming, let me simplify it: start small. One thought. One shift. One action at a time.

Because once you take that first step, everything changes. Not instantly. But eventually. And steadily.

So go forward boldly. Not because it will be easy, but because it will be worth it. The world is waiting for what only you can build. What only you can say. What only you can lead.

You don't have to be perfect. Just present. Just willing. Just brave enough to begin again, one more time.

You've got this.

And we're all better for it.

References

Books and Academic Works:

- Beecher, H. K. (1955). The Powerful Placebo. JAMA.
- Dweck, Carol S. (2006). Mindset: The New Psychology of Success. Random House.
- Frankl, Viktor E. (1946). Man's Search for Meaning. Beacon Press.
- Fredrickson, Barbara L. (2009). Positivity. Crown Publishing Group.
- Hill, Napoleon. (1937). Think and Grow Rich. The Ralston Society.
- Lazar, Sara et al. (2005). Meditation Experience Is Associated with Increased Cortical Thickness. NeuroReport.
- Mischel, Walter. (2014). The Marshmallow Test: Mastering Self-Control. Little, Brown and Company.
- Peale, Norman Vincent. (1952). The Power of Positive Thinking. Prentice Hall.
- Rosenthal, Robert & Jacobson, Lenore. (1968). Pygmalion in the Classroom. Holt, Rinehart & Winston.
- Schultz, Howard. (2011). Onward: How Starbucks Fought for Its Life Without Losing Its Soul. Rodale Books.

Business Leaders, Entrepreneurs, and Public Figures:

- Blakely, Sara. Interviews and talks on entrepreneurship and resilience.
- Carrey, Jim. Public stories and interviews regarding visualization and mindset.
- Chouinard, Yvon. Founder of Patagonia. Referenced in sustainable business case studies.
- Jobs, Steve. Stanford Commencement Address (2005) and various interviews.
- Musk, Elon. Biographical material and media interviews, including Ashlee

Vance's biography.

- Price, Dan. Gravity Payments case study. Coverage from The New York Times, Inc., and other outlets.
- Sethi, Ramit. Author of I Will Teach You To Be Rich, public teachings on personal finance mindset.
- Willingham, Sarah. Business leader insights from The Times and media interviews.
- Winfrey, Oprah. Speeches, interviews, and autobiographical sources.

Spiritual and Philosophical References:

- The Bible. Matthew 17:20, New International Version (NIV).

Productivity and Mindset Tools:

- Cirillo, Francesco. Pomodoro Technique. Time management method.
- Golden, Myron.. Leverage hierarchy and financial growth teachings.
- Robbins, Tony. Public teachings on mindset, peak performance, and entrepreneurship.
- Suinn, Richard. Research on sports visualization and mental rehearsal techniques.

Models and Frameworks Referenced:

- 80/20 Rule (Pareto Principle)
- Eisenhower Matrix (Time and priority management)
- SMART Goals (Specific, Measurable, Achievable, Relevant, Time-bound
- Time Blocking (Productivity technique)
- The "Non-Negotiables" System (Developed by the author)
- 40/70 Rule (General Colin Powell's decision-making model)
- Executive Loneliness (Leadership psychology; Harvard Business Review and others)